UNBECOMING

Letting Go of What No Longer Serves You

Rowen Labuguen Turner

Copyright © 2023 by Rowen Labuguen Turner

All rights reserved. No part of this publication may be reproduced, distributed, or transmitted in any form or by any means including, photocopying, recording, or other mechanical methods, without prior written permission of the Publisher. For permission requests, write to the Publisher, addressed "Attention: Permissions," at the address below or email the Author directly.

This book is presented solely for educational purposes. It is based on my personal journey, insights, and coaching concepts I use for both myself and with clients. As a professional coach and consultant, I am an advocate for coaching and therapy, and I know that many people may have reservations about or face barriers to getting professional help. This book is designed to help bridge that gap as a meaningful first step or complementary tool in self-discovery and holistic health.

There are reflection questions and exercises throughout the book; I encourage you to read this with a journal and pen nearby so you can participate in them.

I am not a licensed therapist, and this book is not intended as a substitute for working one on one with a physician, psychotherapist, qualified clinician, or other professional coach.

ISBN: 9798985619799 (Paperback)
ISBN: 9798985619775 (Hardcover)

Cover by: Aesha Zahra & Avenue K Web Designs
Cover Photo by: Lions Latitude Public Relations & Production

Printed in the United States of America

Robinson Anderson Publishing
2150 S. Central Expressway, Suite 200
McKinney, TX. 75070

Table of Contents

Gratitude	ix
Introduction	xi
Preface: Understanding "Unbecoming"	1
Chapter 1: Our Brain and Unbecoming	7
Chapter 2: Steps to Unbecoming	13
Chapter 3: Our Duality	23
Chapter 4: Owning My Journey	33
Chapter 5: The GAME of Life	39
Chapter 6: Maslow's Hierarchy of Needs	45
Chapter 7: Maslow's Hierarchy and Our Duality	49
Chapter 8: Religion and Self-Transformation	53
Chapter 9: Taking the First Step	59
Chapter 10: Goal Digging	61
Chapter 11: Physiological	69
Chapter 12: Financial Safety	75
Chapter 13: Love and Belonging	87
Chapter 14: Esteem, Career, and Achievement	107
Chapter 15: Self-Actualization and Purpose	119
Further Practice	137
Applying Maslow's Hierarchy to Leadership	147
Applying Maslow's Hierarchy to Business Strategy	153
Unbecoming Reference Material	167
Recommended Reading and Resources	175
About the Author	183

"Maybe the journey isn't so much about becoming anything. Maybe it's about **un-becoming** everything that isn't really you, so you can be who you were meant to be in the first place."
- Paulo Coelho

Dedication

To God, Jesus, the Holy Spirit, Spirit Guides, Angels, Archangels, Ancestors, and All the Forces for Good in the Universe - Thank you for guiding, protecting, providing, and co-creating with me every step of the way.

To the Loves of my Life - Marcus, Myles, and Jett - Thank you for choosing me, being my Joy, and helping me live my Purpose. You are living proof that God exists, and you inspire me to create and serve as big as my faith allows.

To my Parents, Grandparents, and All who came before me - I am endlessly thankful for you and for the sacrifices you made, allowing me the chance to find and live out my Life's Purpose.

To encourage and embolden All who are with me and All who come after me. May you discover and unleash the God within you.

Gratitude

To those who were instrumental in the creation of this book:

Marcus, Sister, Chela, Maryanne, Domo, Noelle, and Latoya - for believing in me and helping me to keep my Vision alive, gain clarity, and for giving life to the Author within me

Nancy and Kalena - for helping me discover the name of my book

Eydie, Hilary, Karletta, Aesha, and the RAPublishing Team - for sharing your wisdom and experience, co-creating with me for God's glory and the good of others, and shifting my Passion to a published work

Lions Latitude - for helping me to amplify my message and expand my impact, and for keeping me confident, having fun, and grounded in myself and my purpose

To those who inspired me in these stories:

My parents and family - for being a constant source of love and encouragement Pastor Sean Sears of Grace Church in Avon, Massachusetts - for helping me make my faith pragmatic

Gaylen Isaacs of Sacred Hearts Academy - for teaching me that progress is a smarter, less stressful, and more enjoyable goal than perfection

Manny, Bikram Yoga Instructor Extraordinaire - for helping me master my mind through my yoga practice

Dennis Niimi of Longs Drugs Hawaii - for teaching me that leaning into my strengths is more powerful than trying to be good at everything

Tim Casey of Longs Drugs Hawaii - for being my first mentor and believing in my talents, giving me opportunities to grow, and inspiring creative ideas

Michael Mushlin - for seeing the Light in me and for sharing your wisdom and Landmark Forum

Maureen Cormier and The Mighty Division 9 of CVS Health - for being the change and for being the most fulfilling part of my last adventure

Tyler Deveraux, Ryan Woolley, Todd Millar, and my MFM and MFCP ohana - for blessing me with the opportunity to align my life's mission with yours

Coach Kendra - for helping me win at all levels in this game of life

All of my mentors and dear friends - for seeing and inspiring the God within me, for supporting me and offering wise counsel, and for challenging me to grow

Introduction

For as long as I can remember, I've always felt my Life Purpose pulling me - calling me to discover it. As a child, this tugging felt like random, fleeting moments of emptiness as I watched adults all around me go through life feeling more busy, tired, and stressed than having fun and enjoying the moment. This left me wondering if "this" - working during the week, taking care of the house and family, and trying to rest and recharge on the weekends - was all that life was about. Somehow as a young girl, I believed and understood there is infinitely more to life than meets the eye.

I consider myself an extremely reflective person who tries to make sense of the world. I enjoy figuring out how faith and religion, science, logic, and theory can work **together** instead of contradicting each other. While the world might focus on explaining one way of thinking over another, I found joy in finding connections. It was like a fun game: discovering the answers to puzzles others would get stumped by or focusing on a detail others couldn't see that was key to understanding a principle. For example, I'd see simple connections in nutritional science and why certain foods, like pork (fat), leave us unclean until the morning, as the Bible asserts. Or I considered much broader topics like the possibility of reincarnation or the role quantum physics plays in the spiritual practices of smudging and manifesting.

Over the last several years, I've been intentional about discovering my meaning in life. This book is a result of my reflections and learnings, both during and after the experiences I've been through. It started as a journal about what I have learned through my life experiences, so I could share and pass it on to my children and their children to help them live more fully. I have a very clear vision of my journal being handed down through generations of my family, my great-great-great-great-great-great grandchildren knowing me intimately, and me being able to assist them through my writing long after I ascend.

Publishing my journal ensures my family has me forever. However, as I prayed, my vision of sharing it with others expanded beyond my family. Publishing my journal also allows me to support as many beings as possible through time by helping them connect to their Spirit self, find fulfillment and attract success by doing the things they love, and discover their Life Purpose. This book provides me with a way to change the world by helping others, regardless of where they are, to Unbecome.

It's taken me four years to find the courage to write and publish this book. The questions and doubts that replayed, and still sometimes replay, in my mind were:

- What stories do I have that are really worth sharing?
- Who will read it?
- Who am I to write a book?
- What will others think of me?
- What criticisms will I receive?

Deep in my spirit, I hear wisdom answering back and empowering me to know that:

- Every person's story matters, including mine.
- Those who are meant to read it will.
- I am whoever I say that I am.
- What others think of me doesn't change who I am.
- We are all different. No two people see and experience everything the exact same way, and that's OK.

Many things I share through this book may not resonate or make sense. It may be because of how I articulate them or simply because it's not a relatable enough situation or perspective for others. I don't have all the answers. I haven't figured it all out. Like many of you, I struggle daily with balancing all the roles and responsibilities I hold, prioritizing taking care of myself, battling imposter syndrome, worrying about having enough money for the future, staying positive when challenges arise, and navigating my way through life's dramas - just to name a few. Our battles may be different, but the methods and exercises I share here can help anyone with whatever difficulties they are having. This is a summary of my experiences. I am vulnerably and authentically sharing with you my journey, my faith, my insights and best practices on how I see life and the world, and how I found my Life Purpose in the hope that it will inspire and help you find your greatest self.

My ultimate intention is spiritual. I pray each of you may come to know or more deeply experience the **spirit and nature** of God (whoever God may be for you), Who is **unconditional, infinite, and divine Love**.

With Love and Gratitude,
 -Rowen

Preface

Understanding "Unbecoming"

"Do not conform any longer to the pattern of this world, but be transformed by the renewing of your mind."

Romans 12:2 New International Version (NIV)

There is a lot of content in the world about becoming our dream selves. We are to become healthier, wealthier, happier, more successful, more loving, and so on. Visually speaking, we can see that there is the person we are today, and then there is the person we are striving to be at some point in the future. The gap in between is the process of becoming that person. The concept of "becoming" can feel overwhelming, and at times, we can feel stuck in the process of not moving forward and even unsure of how to do so. This feeling of being "stuck" usually triggers frustration. However, it may be an indicator that "Unbecoming" is an approach that can assist your transformation. Unbecoming simply serves as a different way to go about growth, especially when you are stalled on your current path.

Becoming is about bringing ourselves forward to a future, desired state. Unbecoming is about bringing ourselves backward, all the way to our child-like state, where there is no fear, worry, or doubt. There is only abundance, possibility, and joy. We Unbecome and bring ourselves back to pure possibility first. Then it's easier to create your new desired state. In fact, when we get really good at Unbecoming and staying in our child-like state, there is no longer a need to become. We are now in a state of possibility where we can just BE - be anything at any given moment, simply because we choose to.

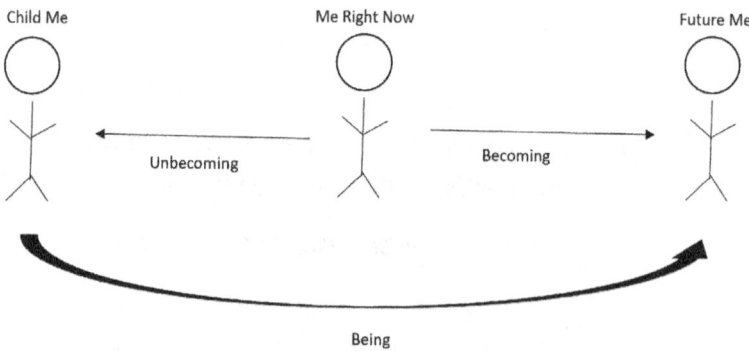

Becoming, Unbecoming, and Being

A fellow coach and friend shared another great visual of the concept with me. Imagine we are a chocolate frosted cake, but we want to change that frosting to vanilla. So, we get some vanilla frosting and put it all over us. But, we don't become a vanilla frosted cake. Instead, we are a chocolate/vanilla frosted swirl cake or a lightly chocolate frosted cake with another layer of vanilla frosting on top. To Unbecome, we must scrape off all the chocolate frosting first to return to being just cake. Only then can we more easily put on whatever flavor of frosting we want and be that flavor. And we can repeat the process for any goal we set for ourselves.

When I think about being in this child-like state and having the ability to be whoever I want to be, I think of a passage in the book of Exodus in the Bible. God refers to himself as "I AM WHO I AM" (Exodus 3:14 [NIV]). The power of that statement was clear to me once I was enlightened to the power that we all have as children: a unique, God-given gift to consciously choose our identity at any given moment. To me, "I AM WHO I AM" speaks to the truth that I AM whoever I believe I AM.

My sons have been my greatest teachers of Unbecoming. I remember a specific "aha" moment that one of them created for me when he was seven months old. It marked the start of my Unbecoming process. It was the morning of April 18, 2018. I was folding laundry on my bed while my son played on the floor near the laundry baskets. Soon, he became aware of and interested in the laundry basket next to him. He proceeded to go to it, grab onto it and attempt to use it to pull himself up to stand. He could not stand well on his own at that age, so I could foresee him falling, along with the empty laundry basket, if he were to put his full weight on it. I watched him from afar with some angst, and as I opened my mouth to warn him of the danger of what he was doing, I noticed the opposite feeling in him, and it caused me to pause. I recall this moment happening in slow motion for me. Despite my concern that he would hurt himself and wanting to protect him, something happened. I became aware of his wonder and the excitement he embodied as he discovered that he could stand by leveraging the things around him. And that difference in mindset intrigued me. I was so focused on the possibility that he could fall, especially since he had just recently learned to sit on his own, that I almost missed him focusing on exploring his body and the surrounding environment while pushing his limits. He was unconcerned with time, age, or the people around him and believed fully in his capabilities. He was just being, doing, and enjoying life. Whenever he became unstable or fell, he didn't get discouraged or defeated. He had fun trying again and again and was getting better each time. I was humbled by his new awareness. Here I was, an expert at being a finite, limited human being, while my son was an expert at being an infinite, limitless spirit. I joined him on the floor, thanked him for teaching me the lesson, and assisted his attempts to stand while joining his play and wonder.

In the "Visual Cliff" and *From Birth to Five Years: Children's Developmental Progress*, research supports scientists' assertion that we were born with only two fears: the feeling of actively falling and loud noises. All other fears are learned. So, if I somehow trained myself to fear many other things, I could undoubtedly train myself to be fearless once again. While my intent was to protect my son and keep him safe, I was about to inadvertently pass my worries on to him and rob him of his joyful exploration. That morning was a powerful reminder that my experiences and environment had taught me to be more cautious and less courageous. And that approach kept me from embracing life as the adventure it intended to be - a truth most young children haven't yet forgotten.

> *"We are human, so we are naturally flawed. We are not able to attain perfection because perfection is a man-made concept. Perfection is our child-like state. When you see a child not in that state, it means they are already tainted."*
>
> *- Anonymous*

Before we continue, a fact that is critical to share is that Unbecoming is probably the most challenging thing you will ever do in your life. It requires you to kill your current identity and transform. For example, think of the caterpillar that turns into a butterfly. During the pupa metamorphosis phase, a caterpillar wraps itself into a protective structure called a chrysalis or cocoon. The caterpillar structures break down for a couple of weeks, or even up to two years while in its wrappings, and the butterfly structures appear. What emerges is no longer a caterpillar or even a caterpillar disguised as a butterfly. The insect has completely Unbecome and changed its identity from a caterpillar to what is now 100% butterfly.

> *"For a seed to achieve its greatest expression, it must come completely undone. The shell cracks, its insides come out and everything changes. To someone who doesn't understand growth, it would look like complete destruction."*
>
> *-Cynthia Occelli*

Everybody wants to transform, yet only some are willing to do what it takes to go through the process of transformation. Killing your ego or current identity can be the scariest and most challenging part of transformation because it requires absolute vulnerability. Only by being truly open to your flaws and power can you realize that your quality of life remains at the same level because of your actions. Notice how I didn't say the quality of your life at this specific moment in time. Quality of life is a qualitative measure and differs from person to person. It reflects how you feel and think within you rather than what's happening outside of you in any given situation or moment. This is the reason there are so many "successful" people in the world who are not fulfilled or content and still long for more. There are also just as many disadvantaged people in the world who still manage to find joy in life. Everything on the outside is a reflection and manifestation of what is occurring on the inside. We're all dealt a varied hand; everyone struggles. The hand we are dealt in life is not our fault, but it is on us to get ourselves out of situations that do not serve us.

Chapter 1

Our Brain and Unbecoming

"Master your mind. Only then can you master your body and unleash your spirit."

-Rowen Labuguen Turner

Through reading and my personal life experiences, I have learned and come to understand that identity is an incredibly powerful tool in self-development because of how we operate. How we function is based on our identity. However, we may not always know what that is or be open to seeing how our perceived identity differs from our desired identity. Furthermore, not being clear on our identity or understanding who we are can be at the core of our pain because we get torn over even the smallest options or decisions. We are uncertain of what to pick or what decision to make and the consequences that can come from those choices. When we are clear on who we are, decisions become easier because we know the direction we want to go. We are better able to embrace life as it occurs, no matter how good, bad, ugly, or glorious it may be.

Understanding how the brain works with respect to our identity is key to Unbecoming. When looking at the image below from Yunjeong Jang's "Artefacts using human brainwaves," we notice we operate predominantly in Delta brainwave cycles from the womb to two years old. This is the same frequency as during deep sleep (Hall n.p.). Brainwaves are electrical impulses in the brain that have different frequencies. Delta brainwaves have a frequency of less than 3.5 Hz. There is no critical thinking or assigned meaning while we are in this state. We are one with our environment and do not see a separation. I've come to know this state as an energy state. During this phase of life, we are absorbing the energy, quality, and consistency of our surroundings. Whatever is accumulated during that period will be the foundation, if you will, on which our identity is built.

From ages two to six, we transition to a Theta state (4-7 Hz), where we begin to comprehend that we are separate from our environments. A sense of self or ego begins, hence the tendency of children to start saying "mine." This is a hyper-learning state of mind, so it is not a coincidence that when in Theta, imagination is off-the-charts. Additionally, people are in this same frequency while experiencing hypnosis or meditation. Therefore, during this time, we are incredibly impressionable and are likely to accept what we are told as truth and without question. We adjust how we operate with events, experiences, people, and other influences we encounter in our environment in order to survive. This is how and when we unknowingly and inadvertently take on the repeated thought and behavior patterns of our caregivers. It can also influence our brains as they develop and enter the Alpha state by age six.

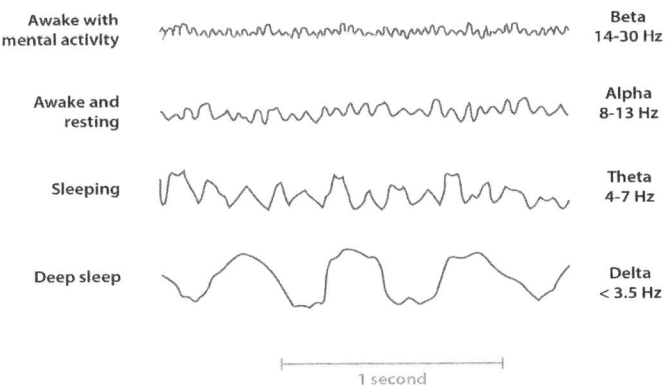

[1]

Before describing the Alpha state, I want to emphasize this point: THIS PERIOD OF EXPERIENCES IS HOW AND WHEN WE UNKNOWINGLY AND INADVERTENTLY TAKE ON THE REPEATED THOUGHT AND BEHAVIOR PATTERNS OF OUR CAREGIVERS. I share this because as I have worked with more clients, I've come to realize that 90%+ of all Americans don't remember what our inner voices sound like. Gaining back the ability to hear our own voice is the most critical part of the process of Unbecoming. We stop listening to our inner voice at an extremely young age. And before we even had conscious awareness of that voice, we had forgotten what it both sounds and feels like. Our inner voice is that part of us that is connected to a higher power. For me, as a Christian, it is connected to God, and I understand it as being the Holy Spirit in me. This is also why meditation is so powerful. It allows us to quiet the mind, zero down the volume on all the other voices we've heard all our lives, and try to hone in on the frequency that is our voice. I know when I finally connect to God, again via the Holy Spirit within me, I will be full of peace and conviction and no longer feel worry or confusion. It takes

---

[1] Yunjeong Jang, "Artefacts using human brainwaves," MA/MFA Computational Arts Blog, Accessed November 1, 2022, http://doc.gold.ac.uk/compartsblog/index.php/work/artefacts-using-human-brainwaves/.

disciplined practice because we must remain consistent with discerning our inner spirit again. And it also takes courage because acknowledging our true Spirit self comes with:

- owning the hurt we've caused ourselves by neglecting our spirit all of these years
- owning the hurt we've caused others because we could only love to the level we have experienced ourselves
- having empathy for others for their imperfections and forgiving their wrongdoings toward us
- killing off our current identities since we have grown incredibly attached to them

OK, back to brain development.

During the ages of five to eight, we begin to have access to the Alpha frequency (8-13 Hz), which is associated with our analytical mind. The awe in this age range is that we are also operating in the Theta state, so we have access to both sides of the brain. It is in this Alpha/Theta state that we are at our best when brainstorming or problem-solving. As adults, we can bring ourselves to this state through deep meditation.

Beta brainwaves kick in from about eight years on, and we enter conscious, logical thinking. We often stay there instead of returning to our Alpha and Theta states, so we can use them when it serves us to do so. For example, meditation is something that I continue to use to work through each state. It helps me to slow my brainwaves. Using mantras or affirmation meditation also activates my Alpha brainwaves. Deep hypnosis can bring them to the Theta state, while mindfulness meditation serves as a gateway to the Delta state. I have also learned that when I am able to clear my mind through meditation, I can better receive insights.

To be able to Unbecome, we must first understand and accept that who we think we are and who we really are, are likely two different beings. How we see ourselves and how we factually show up are often different because our perception is clouded by our filters and emotions. To add another level of complexity, because life is intentionally mysterious, we may not even know who we really are because we learn to live for and please the expectations of others by age two.

On a separate note, this concept has me sold on investing in mothers, caregivers, and children at an early age. I shared how our brains are almost fully developed by six years old. So for me, investing more in a child's environment when they are younger makes sense. Knowing this, it's almost shocking that our education system works in the absolute reverse. We invest more in our children's education when we know there's a lower return on our resources, which in this case is after their brains have fully developed. Please don't misunderstand me. High School and College Education can absolutely be valuable, especially if the field we want requires a degree. I've learned that the highest value we get from a school at any level is the energy quality of the environment and network of people we are surrounded by. When I say energy quality, I mean the predominant emotions and corresponding energy frequency of a person or place. For instance, there can be high-pressured, stressful, and unsafe environments along with joyful, fun, and safe environments. When a child is constantly immersed in a specific kind of emotion or energy frequency, they are not only taught but also gain a predisposition for that kind of emotion or energy. The energy quality and network of people are two reasons why I am a huge proponent of fully funded childcare for all children six weeks to six years to set children up for success in life. By placing our energies here, our children will be better prepared to Unbecome and/or have less Unbecoming to do when they are adults.

To recap, there are two concepts that we need to remain focused on in order to begin the process of Unbecoming. They are:

1. Who we think we are and who we really are, are likely two different beings.
2. We may not even have a clue who we really are.

So, we begin the Unbecoming journey here - by figuring out who we really are and reconnecting with our child-like selves because that identity is still inside us. It might be buried deep and tangled in some cluster of emotions and past traumas. However, it is still there, enthusiastically and patiently waiting for us to find the courage to reunite with it. It takes immense courage because we have to face those emotions and past traumas trapped within us.

However, I share this piece of hope. The possibility, freedom, and joy we unlock when we can consciously be present like we were when we were little are absolutely worth the pain and effort of this self-discovery. Imagine for a moment what that would actually feel like: to have no worry or stress, but only excitement and joy, just because. Now take that feeling you're thinking of and know that BEING UNBECOME feels at least 100 times better than that!!!! So, if you've ever thought you were BEING something, but didn't have that out-of-this-world, exhilarated feeling, know there is still work to be done. So, let's get to it!

Chapter 2

Steps to Unbecoming

As I've shared, Unbecoming is a way to go about growth when you are stalled on your current path. It's about bringing ourselves backward, all the way to our child-like state, where there is no fear or worry, or doubt. I've broken down Unbecoming into four steps. I call them steps to keep it simple. Ideally, you conquer them in this order. However, balancing all four "spiritual" components simultaneously gets challenging because of our human nature, so it's normal to revisit these if you feel a gap.

Step One: Give Yourself Permission to Transform

The first step of Unbecoming is to give ourselves permission to shed our current identity and choose whatever new identity we want. This seems simple enough. However, here is why it is extremely difficult. As physical beings, we are permanently hardwired with the ultimate goal of "don't die." I know that sounds extreme, but certainty, safety, and survival are seen as the ultimate reward. Consequently, we become incredibly attached to our current identity because it works for us and provides us with perceived benefits, results, and rewards. As much as we want to become something else, that new identity is uncharted territory. We perceive it as dangerous because we don't know what to expect. So, we keep our current identity, even if it means staying where we are and not progressing. An additional layer of complexity is that we can get so consumed by our current identity because we've been that person for so long that we forget we can choose and change it at any time. I find this occurs when we are stuck in trying to become. For example, during my whole life, I have strived for perfection or to not fail. Because my identity was anchored in not failing, it took a while for me to choose to become an entrepreneur. I had to Unbecome, be willing to take risks, and be okay with failing. Only then could my identity as an entrepreneur become a real possibility.

Step Two: Embrace our Spirit Nature as Primary

> *"We are not human beings having a spiritual experience. We are spiritual beings having a human experience."*
>
> *- Pierre Teilhard de Chardin*

The second step is to be open to the idea that our mind plays a powerful trick on us. It convinces us to believe that we are physical beings that end when our body dies and not spiritual beings living within our body that will continue to exist and be released when it dies. Once we understand and accept that our true identity is an infinite, divine, and abundant spirit, we will be able to separate ourselves from our finite, worldly, and limited ego and conquer and shed it away.

To illustrate this, I'll share a personal example of when I was stuck trying to "become" and had to "Unbecome" first. I had three goals that were not getting the traction I wanted. They were: 1) writing this book, 2) transforming the culture of Corporate America, and 3) providing safe homes and communities where others can thrive. I was making some movement here and there, but I wasn't consistently crushing it. I reasoned that I didn't have enough time or energy to take action like I wanted because I had a very demanding job, a husband and two young kids that I needed and wanted to spend time with, and an endless list of household chores. Plus, I needed to rest. Even though these were good reasons, I could feel I wasn't being true to myself. I was making excuses. But I couldn't understand why.

After a weekend of deep reflection and meditation, where I focused on trying to break through my hesitation in this area, I saw that my current identity was someone in the background or behind the scenes, like a backup dancer or the Wizard of Oz. I had a lot of pride in this identity because it had been with me for as long as I could remember, and I was successful as the "behind the curtain" person. But, when I considered my dreams and who I needed to be to make those things happen, I noticed the root cause of my stalling was that my three goals demanded I step up from behind the scenes and stand on the stage and in the spotlight. That was frightening because that had never been me. It was the exact opposite of my current identity. I was uncomfortable being "front and center" with all of the attention placed on me. Thinking of being the lead role or star of the show filled me with doubt and made me nervous, faint, and sweaty. But, my authentic self reminded me that if I wanted to achieve those three goals, I had to shed that current identity.

Step Three: Get Clear on Your "Why"

> *"He who has a Why can endure any How."*
>
> -Frederick Nietzsche

Earlier, I shared Cynthia Occelli's quote about what meaningful growth feels like and referenced the caterpillar's metamorphosis into a butterfly. Unbecoming is like this. It is a huge feat. It's not a little change that makes you a bit uncomfortable. Unbecoming is a full transformation, a letting go of everything that no longer serves you. And so you have to be very clear on your "Why," and your "Why" has to be big enough, emotionally moving enough to begin, endure and complete the process and journey. Your "Why" does not have to make sense or energize others. It is sufficient when it ignites you, and you are willing to take necessary and massive action because of it. Your "Why" can be a loved one, an emotional state you crave and long for yourself, or an emotional state you crave and long for someone else.

In the beginning, you'll find your "Why" may be different depending on the goal. As you continue to evolve through life, and if you're intentional about connecting with your Spirit self, you'll begin to see how your "Why" becomes consistent and how each goal becomes an additional way to see it through. When you land on your consistent "Why," you have found your Life Purpose. We will discuss this more in the "Self-Actualization and Purpose" chapter.

Step Four: Leverage Mindset and Beliefs

Figuring out when and how I created my current identity was very helpful in letting it go. I used to think that identities occurred because of big emotionally-charged situations. But, I discovered that sometimes identities are created just because, and there's not a deeper meaning or riveting storyline to match.

Let me elaborate on that. Looking into my past, I saw that my identity as a co-star, or behind-the-scenes person, happened mainly because I was a second child. Being a second child, I looked to my older sister for guidance. She knew more than me and was fun to be around. As most younger siblings do, I followed in her footsteps. Because of this dynamic, the concept of following someone else's lead or tagging along was reinforced daily, so much so that it subsequently became a key part of my identity. As a creature that adapts to my surroundings, I found a way to succeed with that identity. Yet, I wanted to take on leadership roles, starting as young as eight years old. Still, looking back, I realized I gravitated towards the second-in-command type of positions and shied away from the lead roles all throughout elementary school and high school. Career-wise, while I've had great success as an HR leader, I usually supported the Operator. And even in romantic relationships, I found myself with men who were in the spotlight, which allowed me to stay safe in my comfort zone as a "co-pilot." Behind the scenes was where I had grown to be comfortable and impactful.

It's often not easy or simple to change behaviors that are associated with a specific, desired state because the beliefs that drive those behaviors don't necessarily align with them. When we find we are not getting traction on changing our behaviors or habits, we might find a breakthrough in changing our beliefs and mindset. Early in my career, I was taught that our mindset drives how we behave, and how we behave determines the results we get. I've leveraged this principle in every area of my life. We often focus on the results and behaviors we want and don't focus enough on our thinking or, more specifically, our mindset or beliefs. Allow me to explain further.

Let's say there are two people who both want to lose ten pounds in six months. They meet with a nutritionist and dietician, who recommends a weekly exercise plan to eliminate all junk food-type snacks. Six months later, Person A reaches her goal, but Person B does not. When asked how she reached her goal, Person A enthusiastically replied, "I followed the plan! It was hard, and I was tempted many times, but I really wanted to lose the weight, so I stuck with it." When Person B was asked why she didn't reach her goal, she shared, "I didn't follow the plan. Well, I followed it for a week, and then it got more difficult. Work got more stressful, and I snack and eat more when I'm stressed, and then there were days I was tired, so I didn't work out."

This is a very simplified example, but we see here that the result was different because not only were the behaviors different, but their mindset and what they were focusing on were different as well. If I were Person B's coach, I'd share the observations that: 1) staying stressed and being comfortable appears to mean more to her than losing ten pounds, and 2) she quits when things get hard. She might get offended and attempt to convince herself that's not true. But the hard reality is if losing ten pounds meant more to her than giving in to her stress and being comfortable, and if she had kept pushing, even when things got hard, then she would have stuck with the eating and exercise plan to meet her goal.

An exercise I find powerful in having a breakthrough with a new habit is identifying the driving mindset or belief that reinforces the behavior, so you can get yourself to believe it. Then, it becomes easier to do.

For example, let's say I want to change how I approach the start of my day. What current behaviors or habits contribute to my being tired when I wake up, and how can I change them? The following exercise can help me to identify those behaviors and implement a change.

Achieving a Desired Goal

	Current State	**Desired State**
Outcome	I feel tired in the morning and want to sleep in.	I want to feel amazing in the morning and feel like I can conquer the world!
Proven Action/Habit	Get 4-6 hours of sleep at night. Go to bed whenever I'm done watching TV and browsing my social media accounts.	Get 8 hours of sleep at night. Go to bed by 10 pm during the week and watch TV shows and surf social media only on the weekends.
Driving Mindset/ Belief	I care more about staying caught up with my TV show and what's on social media than I do my well-being.	Being well-rested helps me to be my best and have a productive day at work and home. That matters more than staying caught up on my TV show and what's on social media.

What's a goal you have for yourself and want to achieve? What habits or behaviors can you change to reach that goal? On the next page, there are a few grids you can use to do this exercise yourself. Complete the grids with one or two of your Desired Goals to lead you on your path to Unbecoming. You can do this exercise whenever you set a goal or feel stuck achieving it.

Desired Goal #1

	Current State	Desired State
Outcome		
Proven Action/ Habit		
Driving Mindset/ Belief		

Desired Goal #2

	Current State	Desired State
Outcome		
Proven Action/ Habit		
Driving Mindset/ Belief		

The power of this exercise lies in being matter-of-fact and identifying the driving mindset or belief behind your current and desired actions and habits. It allows you the opportunity to become aware of your subconscious mindset or beliefs, then willfully choose which one best serves you toward the quality of life you truly desire. For instance, in the previous example, you are left to choose between the Driving Mindset/Belief of the Current State and that of the Desired State.

Also, please know that even if you choose your current state, the exercise is still incredibly valuable because now you are in an empowered position to understand that you have chosen to remain in your situation. You cannot succumb to a victim mentality or embrace the excuse that you remain there due to forces outside of your control or influence. When you own the fact you always have the choice to operate one way or another, it becomes harder to blame other people or instances for an outcome you're not content with.

You'll know you've successfully completed this exercise when you can review what you wrote in the grid. The goal or scenario that used to feel complex now feels simple and clear. The work lies in which mindset or belief you willfully and consciously take on for yourself. Once you've completed this exercise with a goal that is meaningful to you, take some time to reflect on what you've discovered about yourself.

Reflection Question: What mindsets or beliefs do you have that serve your current identity but you need to let go of and change to serve your desired identity?

The last thought I want to cover about our brains and Unbecoming is that we are unique from all other beings on this earth in that we have the power to CO-CREATE this universe with God and each other. No other being can come up with any idea, intentionally choose to focus energy on it, and take persistent and relentless action toward that vision to make it a reality. This is an incredible power and ability that God has given us. The saying goes, "With great power, comes great responsibility," which is true in this case. (Benjamin Parker, *Spiderman*, 2002) We have the responsibility to use this power for good and for the progress of all mankind. Our power is always on, so if it's not being intentionally used for good, then know we are allowing it to be used otherwise. Staying stagnant or being distracted is a waste and shows our lack of understanding and appreciation for this gift.

> *"Watch your thoughts, they become your words;*
> *watch your words, they become your actions;*
> *watch your actions, they become your habits;*
> *watch your habits, they become your character;*
> *watch your character, it becomes your destiny."*
>
> *– Lao Tzu*

Chapter 3

Our Duality

In the earlier section, I shared Pierre Teilhard de Chardin's assertion that "We are not human beings...We are spiritual beings" that live inside a temporary human body. The human part of us has an unyielding stronghold because we are currently experiencing living in a physical body. So, it's easy to focus on our human side since it is also a physical part of this world. Thus, this stronghold impacts all five of our senses because that is how we interact with this world. It has a surround-sound pull, and we are easily deceived into thinking that the human part of us is our true nature when in reality, it is our spiritual side.

However, my experience has been that we exist as a duality. We are two beings in one: a Spirit being, which is our true nature, and a Human being which, simply put, is the packaging we, as spirits, come in. But, we can only behave as one of these identities at any given moment. So we must set a new goal: in each moment, we must learn to master our minds and bodies, resist the surround-sound triggers to behave as Human, and choose our Spirit identity and behave in that manner.

Consider it this way: We are not our cars; we ride in our cars. We are not our homes; we live in our homes. We are not our clothes; we wear our clothes. While this seems straightforward and easy to understand right now, there are many moments in life when we forget this. We draw very strong connections with our identities and even define them with the kind of car we drive, the size, value, or location of our home, and the brand of clothes we wear. And by doing this repeatedly, we reinforce to our brains that we are Human, thereby inadvertently telling our brains to forget our Spirit identity. This is because our brains generally operate based on the beliefs we are raised with if we haven't done conscious work on our belief system. The predominant beliefs are what our brains will see as truth.

One way I can assess the extent to which I am grounded in the belief that I am a Spirit first is how I feel and what I focus on whenever someone I care about passes away. Now, I know that I will likely always feel loss and grief when someone I love dies because I am Human, and I feel pain when anything I'm attached to disappears. However, once I remember that I am Spirit first, I find peace as I nurture my belief that I didn't really lose that person because their Spirit and energy cannot be destroyed. Physicists Albert Einstein and Rudolf Clausius assert this principle through their Law of Conservation of Energy and First Law of Thermodynamics, respectively.

The Law of Conservation of Energy states energy cannot be created or destroyed. The First Law of Thermodynamics states energy is, thus, transferred from one form to another. I believe those who've gone before are still here and present with us, just without a human body we can see or touch. With each death I experience, I see it as an opportunity to get more grounded in this truth.

Who we choose to be in any given moment can be identified in the following Two Main Identities grid. When we embody or act in alignment with the left-hand column, we reinforce our Spirit self. When we embody or act in alignment with the right-hand column, we reinforce our Human self.

Two Main Identities	
Spirit	**Human**
Authentic	Inauthentic
Divine	Worldly
Infinite	Finite
Live	Exist/Don't Die
Love	Lust/Control
Giving/Service	Getting/Ego
Create	Consume
Needs	Wants
Abundance	Scarcity
Win-Win/Collaboration	Win-Lose/Competition
Gratitude	Jealousy
Forgiveness	Offense
Security	Insecurity
Faith - Focus on the Promise; Embrace Struggle	Fear - Focus on the Pain; Avoid Struggle
Peace	Pain/Suffering
Lifted/Free	Weighed Down/Tethered
Joy (Intrinsic)	Happiness (Extrinsic)
Adventure	Safety
Awe/Wonder of the "Ordinary"	Increased Stimulation
Progress	Perfection
Growth Mindset	Fixed Mindset
Emotional Feeling (Internal)	Five Senses (External)
Impact	Achievement
Holy	Healthy
Present Moment & Energy	Money

The comparison between the two identities is pretty straightforward. You'll notice how some pairs are exact opposites of each other, like Authentic and Inauthentic or Infinite and Finite. Other pairs are not necessarily exact opposites but more so complementary forces, like yin and yang. Here are a few notable distinctions that may not be intuitive, so I want to unpack them a bit more.

- **Create vs. Consume:** Our Spirit identity is the part of us that uses Theta brainwaves, which we primarily use when we are two to six years old. Thus, when we are our Spirit selves, we are wildly imaginative and creative. We can see solutions that others don't and create them for the good of others. But in our Human identity, we are focused on survival and acquiring the things we need to survive. Thus, we are focused on consuming.
- **Faith vs. Fear:** The term faith is often used to refer to a specific religion. In this context, however, I prefer its other definition, as defined by *Oxford Languages,* of having "complete trust or confidence in … something". I classify faith in reference to our choice to use our brain power to focus on the possibility of a positive future instead of a negative one. I look to embrace that future rather than fear it.
- **Lifted/Free vs. Weighed Down/Tethered:** It is natural for humans to worry and plan for the future or to hold on to things in the past. This is what causes the feeling of weight or being limited. We don't even realize the weight we carry or hold on to because we have grown used to it. It is usually hiding in our blind spots. Only when we can perceive the things we are holding onto can we choose to release them and become completely free to experience the wonder and awe in everything. Like a child, we Unbecome and are lifted from the weight.
- **Joy vs. Happiness:** I hear a lot about how we strive to be happy. While happiness is positive, it is limited because it depends on an external factor like a reward, success, or pleasant surprise that

we don't necessarily have control over because that factor exists outside of ourselves. So, relying solely on happiness can cause unnecessary suffering because the next reward, success, or pleasant surprise might not come when we want it or in the way we want it. Instead, I choose to delve further and strive for joy, which has an internal source. I describe joy as happiness on steroids. It runs deeper and soars higher than happiness. When I feel joy, there is a deeper connection to my Spirit, and it usually comes with immense gratitude for others as well. I feel happy after having had a fun day off, eating a great meal, or passing a test. I feel joy when I connect with my husband, see how much my boys feel loved by us, or help a stranger in need and provide them with renewed hope for the future.

- **Awe/Wonder vs. Stimulation:** Awe and wonder are additional traits that also align with the Theta brainwave state. We notice it in young children when they see bubbles or a toy for the first time, and they are utterly amazed and fully content in their awe of it. However, once we grow older and become adults, we become numb to the wonder of everyday miracles and can even take them for granted. We rely on stimulation in ever-increasing amounts to feel alive. For example, I remember being in high school and starting to have friends and acquaintances who used drugs. I usually did not take issue with their decision to use substances so long as they didn't try to pressure me to do so. As a teenager, I recall being intrigued by the science of chemical substances. After all, they were man-made chemicals we could consume and create chemical reactions in our brains and bodies. They could artificially unlock a state of awe and wonder. I was sixteen or seventeen when I challenged myself to create a life where I could be in awe and wonder whenever I wanted. I didn't know exactly how to do this, but I've since discovered it's within us to be fully present at any given moment. And that ability allows us to control and access the state of awe and wonder for ourselves.

- **Impact vs. Achievement:** Impact is about focusing more on the effect we have on others instead of getting a specific outcome from them. Achievement focuses more on obtaining an outcome than the effect that outcome will have on others, even if it's at their expense. This can be a simple comparison to understand. However, it is often a challenging distinction to see within our own thinking, particularly with people who are high performing and have a strong drive toward specific outcomes.

Let's take another look at the identity grid. For each pair of characteristics, circle the word that most consistently describes you in the past few weeks. This exercise will provide an awareness of which identity you are choosing to reinforce. Now, here's the good news - the perfect answer is the honest one. I don't believe it's possible to reach the Spirit state 100% of the time, so long as we still have a physical body. So, if you have more circles in the Spirit column, then you likely make an intentional effort to be your Spirit self. Suppose you have more circles in the Human column. In that case, you are now aware of the identities you need to focus on and have the power to choose differently going forward.

Two Main Identities	
Spirit	**Human**
Authentic	Inauthentic
Divine	Worldly
Infinite	Finite
Live	Exist/Don't Die
Love	Lust/Control
Giving/Service	Getting/Ego
Create	Consume
Needs	Wants
Abundance	Scarcity
Win-Win/Collaboration	Win-Lose/Competition
Gratitude	Jealousy
Forgiveness	Offense
Security	Insecurity
Faith - Focus on the Promise; Embrace Struggle	Fear - Focus on the Pain; Avoid Struggle
Peace	Pain/Suffering
Lifted/Free	Weighed Down/Tethered
Joy (Intrinsic)	Happiness (Extrinsic)
Adventure	Safety
Awe/Wonder in the "Ordinary"	Increased Stimulation
Progress	Perfection
Growth Mindset	Fixed Mindset
Intuition (Internal)	Five Senses (External)
Impact	Achievement
Holy	Healthy
Present Moment & Energy	Money

Reflection Question: How often do you choose to be your Spirit or Human self? Are there instances where it is easier or harder for you to choose your Spirit self over your Human self?

We lose sight of who we are as Spirits and the freedom we have to choose a different behavior at any given moment. It is easier to choose our Human self and let our current habits keep us from our goals. As I understand it, every moment in life is an opportunity for us to choose who we are. Consequently, the version of ourselves that we consistently and persistently choose at each moment adds up to who we become in the future. And while we can choose to be either Human or Spirit, the end goal is to choose Spirit and experience the AWE, WONDER, and CREATIVE POWER of what it means to embrace our Spirit while in Human form.

I find the concept is extremely similar to what we see in tending a garden. Everything we do within our environment has some bearing on nurturing the fruits, vegetation, and flowers we are trying to grow. If we act as our Spirit selves, we will grow a fruitful and abundant garden. If we act as our Human selves, then we grow a garden that is limited and uncertain. While we don't always have complete control over the kind of environment we are living in, we are still 100% responsible, whether we like it or not, for growing the best garden we can with what we have. If it doesn't grow how we want it to, we sometimes complain about or ignore our garden, which will only nurture a garden of weeds. And if we continue to complain and choose to not look deeper at why our garden isn't growing, the result will be a desolate garden.

It's also easy to forget growing a garden takes time. Some may understand this, while others may feel triggered because they already feel "behind time." May I share with you a powerful truth? Time is simply a measurement, but we attach so much unnecessary meaning to it. I believe what is more powerful to understand is *before* and *after* the order of events. Time compels us to obsess about pace and how quick or slow we are to get results compared to others.

To build further on this "life is a garden we grow" analogy, it is common to ask: "What is the point of growing a garden? Will I be selling or giving away what I grow? Is there a quota on how much should be grown and the variety of fruits, vegetables, and flowers in my garden? What do other gardens look like? Will my garden be pretty and/or functional? What resources will I be given to grow my garden?" I've discovered that while it is natural to have these concerns, we should not focus on just those kinds of questions. The intent behind growing a garden is to help us realize our innate power as Gardeners: to cultivate or destroy life so that by the time this experience is complete for us, we might learn how to harness that power and create for the good of others. Thus, the intent is two-fold: 1) to help us grow ourselves, the most important beings in our life's garden, then 2) to give of ourselves and help others grow their own garden. The game-changing insight for me was when I began to understand and own the very difficult reality that my garden - the quality of my life - was, in fact, a reflection of the condition inside myself. While it was not a reflection of my self-worth or potential, it was simply and factually a reflection of my ability to choose my Spirit self over my Human self over and over again at any given moment. I encourage you to consider this and practice choosing it for yourself.

This same principle is similarly captured in the Cherokee "Legend of The Two Wolves." This fable has many variations, but I would like to share with you the version that affected me the most, as found on Flora Tan's website, A-Simple-Christian.com :

> *One evening, an elderly Cherokee brave told his grandson about a battle that goes on inside people. 'My dear one, the battle between two 'wolves' is inside us all. One is evil. It is anger, envy, jealousy, sorrow, regret, greed, arrogance, self-pity, guilt, resentment, inferiority, lies, false pride, superiority and ego. The other is good. It is: joy, peace, love, hope, serenity, humility, kindness, benevolence, empathy, generosity, truth, compassion and faith.' The grandson thought about it for a moment and then asked his grandfather, 'Which wolf wins?' The old Cherokee replied, 'The one you feed.'*[2]

---
2 "Two Wolves - A Cherokee Story - also known as Grandfather Tells and The Wolves Within," A-Simple-Christian.com, accessed November 1, 2022, https://www.a-simple-christian.com/two-wolves.html.

Reflection Question: If, at the end of our lives, we each leave behind a garden, what kind of garden would make you incredibly proud? Tomorrow isn't promised, so what kind of gardener are you today?

Chapter 4

Owning My Journey

"Blessed is the one who stays awake and remains clothed, so as not to go naked and be shamefully exposed."

-Revelation 16:15 (NIV)

When I look back on my childhood, I see two foundational aspects of my identity stemming from my being a second-generation Filipino-American - obedience and overwhelming pressure to get all A's in school. These beliefs have been so valuable to me. They helped me develop high emotional intelligence, superior relationship-building skills, and excellent reasoning and critical thinking skills. They also limited me in certain respects. Speaking up when I have a different opinion from others and obsessing about the letter grade I received over what I learned in a class marked the beginning of me burying my authentic Spirit self and settling on my Human identity, with a strong tendency to please others.

I mentioned earlier that I grew up Catholic. For as long as I can remember, I went to church every Sunday. My parents were disciplined about attending Mass weekly, and I am grateful they gave me God and my Faith because I now see it as the most important gift to give to children. My mom and dad both worked extremely hard and made many joint and individual sacrifices to put my sister, brother, and me through Catholic school. I went to church less frequently in college because my weekends were filled with work or friends. But because of my childhood, I had a strong knowledge of Catholic and Christian teachings. And while I had learned and memorized Scripture and doctrine, I realized I had only scratched the surface level of their meaning.

Having this strength and faith in God, given to me by my parents, helped me when I hit the lowest point in my life in the Spring of 2008. Thankfully, it also marked the beginning of my own Unbecoming. But it wasn't easy. To be fully transparent with you, I want to share what my life was like during this extremely vulnerable time.

I had finally ended things with my then-boyfriend, who I was convinced was "the one." I had invested an imbalanced amount of time, energy, and resources into growing that relationship and helping him reach his career goals instead of focusing on my own relationship with myself. And so when it was over, I felt like I had nothing. I was an hourly pharmacy technician, struggling with getting into Pharmacy School because my undergraduate GPA had dropped below 2.0. Those who know me might be in shock reading this because I had always been extremely studious in school and was used to having top grades. Additionally, I had accumulated over $35,000 in credit card debt. I used money to distract myself and remained in a state of denial by buying material things and going on trips to make myself feel like I was better off than I actually was.

As a result, I was incredibly embarrassed to admit that these were the unfortunate consequences I was experiencing in my life. And more importantly, I was blind to the fact that I was the one responsible for them. So, I played the blame game. I blamed my ex-boyfriend for letting me invest more time and money in his career than in my own. I blamed my college for allowing me to graduate with a GPA that was too low to get into any of their graduate programs. I blamed pharmacy schools for not seeing my potential and not giving me a chance. I blamed my parents for not letting me explore my interests more when I was younger so that I would know what I wanted to do and not feel lost. I didn't want to accept that while there were external factors that came into play, it was ultimately my sole responsibility to respond to my situation. It was up to me to either accept it and stay in that space or to acknowledge it, own it, and change it. I was worried and stressed I wouldn't be able to rise above this mess that I had put myself in. I was paralyzed with fear of having failed my parents and wasted the money they spent on my private school and college education.

In the beginning, there were more moments of fear and doubt than faith and conviction. What helped me to get myself together and take action for my circumstances was this faint yet ever-present reminder of the dreams God had placed in my heart. At the time, there wasn't any detail to my dreams. For example, I couldn't see what my career should be. There was just an understanding and belief, deep in my Spirit, that I was capable of and destined for more than what I had created out of my life to date. I definitely wanted more out of life than what I had at that time. So, I made the decision to choose courage: to own my journey, to take responsibility for my mistakes, and to forgive myself. I began to sacrifice daily distractions in the short term and do everything I could toward positive, sustained progress for my future.

In order to do this, I set specific goals. My first three goals were to: 1) wake up each day, stay encouraged and not feel defeated daily, 2) get out of debt and transform my relationship with money, and 3) identify a career to pursue. In order to get started, I needed to break down each of these goals and set a path toward completing them.

Goal #1: Wake Up Each Day and Stay Encouraged

Regarding this first goal, I knew I had to find a way to not feel defeated each and every day. Thanks to my upbringing, I knew that faith and focusing on my relationship with God was the key. Since I was at my lowest point, I constantly prayed to God during this period in my life. I thanked Him for not giving up on me and asked for His continued help and guidance through this storm. Even with all that prayer, it was still very easy to be anxious about my finances and future, to have doubt that I could accomplish my goals, and to feel overwhelmed by how tired I was and how much work I still had ahead of me to bring this all to life.

One night in 2009, while eating dinner after a long day of work, I was channel surfing and came across Joel Osteen on the television. For so many years, I had flipped past his show whenever it'd come up, but for some reason, on this night, I decided to stop and listen. His style of preaching and the positive energy he created through the delivery of his words captivated me. His sermon was the perfect balance of everyday, motivational logic and Bible-based wisdom. I felt a level of encouragement, excitement, and hope that I had never felt before. I was inspired to include his sermons in my daily routine and listen to him regularly to keep my spiritual energy strong and remain in command of my mind.

In that episode, Joel posed this powerful reflection question that grounded me even further in this concept of "owning my journey":

"If you don't feel as close to God as you used to, who moved?"

At that moment, I was humbled by the realization that it was me who moved away from God. I had been blindly idolizing being in a relationship with my ex-boyfriend over being in one with God. I had stopped putting God first and had started putting my earthly relationships as a main priority in my life.

Owning my journey means that I recognize and take seriously the power God has given me to create my life experience, no matter what my circumstance is. For every bad scenario I run into and let define me, there is at least one other person who has encountered the same, if not worse, scenario and has chosen to grow through it. And I knew that I could do it too. With this new resolve, I also learned that the low points in our lives are not bad. The way I see it, the low points make the high points, and even the plateaus, more miraculous.

Let me share a simple example with you to explain this in greater detail. When I lived in Hawaii, my Bikram Yoga instructor would give us iced washcloths to help cool our faces and bodies down after being in a 105-degree room steamed with 40% humidity for ninety minutes. Now, everyone who has taken a Bikram class knows that getting to have a simple iced washcloth at that moment was absolute bliss! But, it would not have felt as wonderful and amazing as it did had it not been for the hard work I had put in right before receiving it.

Goal #2: Get Out of Debt and Transform My Relationship With Money

At the core of financial freedom is an awareness that, regardless of its power, money is not a master. While many blindly fall into the mental and emotional prison of worshiping and desiring money, the truth is WE are its master, and it can be a tool for doing good in this world. But we will only be able to become debt-free and achieve our financial goals once we come to this realization. I will cover more on this goal in greater detail on how to get out of debt in the "Financial Safety" chapter of the book.

Goal #3: Identify a Career to Pursue

When it comes to a Career or Life Purpose, our Human nature reinforces us to do what our parents or caregivers want us to and follow the money. It is not always easy to recall our inner voice and remember what we once wanted since we've ignored it for many years. Whether we are mindful of it or not, when we were children, we knew our gifts and the career we wanted to pursue. It is up to us to remember those gifts to obtain that career. I will share more about this process and how to achieve this goal in the "Esteem, Career, and Achievement" chapter.

Ask yourself: what will be the first three goals you pick to begin your transformation towards your Spirit self and Unbecoming? They may not be the same as mine since you should choose goals you feel are right for your journey. However, I believe the goals you pick for yourself will align with Maslow's Hierarchy of Needs, which we will discuss later in the book. For example, they should be physiological and/or provide financial safety, love, and belonging. Owning your journey is necessary to Unbecome because this full ownership of your current quality of life will give you the power to change it.

Chapter 5

The GAME of Life

Believe it or not, life is a game - the GREATEST GAME of all time! I don't mean it's trivial or insignificant or that it should be too serious and intense with the need to win. It is designed to be enjoyable and fun. As detailed earlier, it is absolutely designed that way for us when we are babies and children. And at varying points, we learn how to be Human. We learn to pick the Human version of ourselves more frequently when we share experiences with others and undergo events and emotions while understanding more about this world.

My boys help me be aware of when I've stopped playing and having fun so I can choose to rejoin them. For example, there are times when I'll be in a rush trying to pack up everything to get us out of the house as quickly as possible because we are already behind schedule. I begin to feel impatience and irritation creep inside me, which triggers negative thoughts and judgment. Eventually, raising my voice or yelling begins:

- "Hurry up!"
- "You guys are so slow!"
- "Ugh - I can't wait for you to be older and take care of yourself!"

- "Why don't you understand we have to be somewhere right now?"
- "I'm the only one who ever cares that we have to get things done."

So first, let me say to all of my Moms out there - raise your hand if you can relate to these thoughts I've played out in my head. Perhaps you've also said them out loud to your loved ones. Second, how did you feel after you said them?

What I've trained myself to do when I feel that impatience and irritation appear is to pause and remember that I should be following my sons' lead. Even this type of small instance where I am being mindful of my behavior to bring myself back to my child-like state is a big step in Unbecoming. I focus on being in and making the most of the present moment. I coach myself to resist any temptation to make the situation any worse than it is by playing out all the worst-case scenarios in my head. After that, I can now consider other scenarios based on how I am feeling:

- So what if we're late?
- So what if things don't go exactly according to my plan?
- Is it really the end of the world?
- How can I remain joyful at this moment simply because I choose to?

Pausing comes naturally now, but it didn't for a long time. In fact, in the beginning, I could go from 0 to 1,000 instantly. However, with discipline and practice, immediate rage became less frequent and lessened into anger. Soon, the anger weakened to just feeling bothered or upset. Eventually, it came to a point where I didn't feel any sense of negativity at all. Despite the craziness around me, I could even laugh at the moment and stay in peace and joy. While I simplified the evolution I experienced, it was a very challenging transition. Harboring and fostering negative emotions is so appealing to our Human nature because it is strongly connected to our fight or flight response, which is designed to keep us alive.

A key breakthrough I had in this area was hearing a sermon by Pastor Sean Sears of Grace Church in Avon, Massachusetts. This is a summary of what he shared:

> *When we squeeze oranges, orange juice comes out. When we squeeze lemons, lemon juice comes out. Lemon juice never comes out of oranges. Orange juice never comes out of lemons.*

It seems obvious, yet this is a profound concept. Only that which is inside of something can come out. Too often, we blame our triggers or others for the mess that comes from us. However, we are the ones responsible because these negative emotions must exist within us first in order for them to come out when pressured. While we can't control other people or events from triggering us, we have absolute control over what we hold inside us - the true condition and nature of our hearts. It was pivotal for me to first discover, own, and then face the rage that I held and allowed to unknowingly enter and grow in my heart. Once I accomplished this, I could let it go and replace it with love.

> *"Above all else, guard your heart, for everything you do flows from it."*
>
> *-Proverbs 4:23 (NIV)*

Another way this GAME of life stops feeling fun is when we try to play it without God. We, as Humans, have gotten so good at finding ways to have a perfect life that we've mapped that life out for ourselves and strived to live it. We obey our parents, listen to our teachers, and get good grades in school to get a good-paying job. We do this so that we can have the resources to cover or prevent any negative situation or inconvenience that may come our way. The fear of things not going our way inadvertently causes us to protect our Human selves and therefore remain within our Human identity while experiencing a limited life. We convince ourselves that this world is flawed and bad and that unfair things will happen. And it is easy to live and stay in that fear.

The good news is that when we invite God in to help us see beyond the storm, we start to shift our focus from fear to the promises and great plans He has for our life. He helps us grow and remember the good within us, whether that be love, intelligence, strength, empathy, or wisdom. God is a strong partner in our Unbecoming; He helps us remove the "learned" fear we have so we can get back to our child-like state, our Spirit selves.

I use a memory of an experience I had at the 50th State Fair as an analogy to help me keep life fun and enjoyable while also keeping God close. When I was young, I looked forward to going to the State Fair at Aloha Stadium with my cousins every summer. I remember walking through the fairgrounds wanting to see and try everything, even when I was sometimes afraid to try the bigger rides. I also remember that whenever I heard my older cousins remind me we had thirty minutes left before we had to leave, I was quickly able to prioritize what I wanted to accomplish in those thirty minutes. And I somehow found the courage to ride the biggest and scariest ride I had avoided until the end. I think the same thing happens with life. There is a freedom and power in being fully present. If we can genuinely get grounded in the fact that time is limited and tomorrow is not promised, only then will we be better able to gain clarity of what is paramount so we can do the things that matter most, no matter how uncomfortable they may make us feel.

To further understand the freedom and power of being fully present, take a few moments to answer the following questions:

Reflection Question: If you knew you would physically die 24 hours from now, how would you fill those 24 hours?

Reflection Question: Now that you are clearer on what is most important to you right now, how can you apply this wisdom to each day going forward?

I'd like to share an additional insight regarding time. Thinking that we are "short on time" or "behind schedule" and, thus, won't be able to do everything we need or want to do can cause a large part of our stress and worry. However, I have come to discover that this lens is not real because we were never meant to do every single thing that we think we want to do. When we practice Unbecoming, it gets easier to get past the constraints we allow time to put upon us and learn that the concept of a date and time is an illusion. There is only before and after in the Spiritual realm. With every dream God places in our hearts, there is a series of next steps and lessons to discover in order to get to the glory God has for us. That's why there are many times when we are in lockstep with Him. We are "in the zone," where things can happen faster or take longer because, ultimately, it's not about a date. It's about the specific, clear journey He's custom designed for each of us. Once we come to terms with this, we can find joy, peace, and freedom in knowing that God can make EVERYTHING work out to our advantage.

In this Game of Life, your destiny is yours and only yours. No one can take it from you. There is always a reason for the timing, but we must recognize it in order to make it work.

> *"We are confident that God is able to orchestrate everything to work toward something good and beautiful when we love Him and accept His invitation to live according to His plan."*
>
> -Romans 8:28 The Voice Bible (VOICE)

Now that you've considered what is most important to you, let me end this chapter with a statement I've experienced as fact: **Life is NOT dangerous or scary when we CHOOSE to see it that way.**

At this point, many of you are likely thinking that I'm removed from reality. Just turn on the TV, Rowen, and you'll see you're wrong. People, even kids, are dying every day. Some in extremely unfair ways. I really wish I had all the answers to explain that.

But everything in life is a choice. We are creators who can create whatever reality we want, both consciously and subconsciously, through the powerful stories we repeatedly tell ourselves. But we can choose each next chapter and the ending of our stories. Looking again at the question above, where we ask ourselves what we would do if we had just one more day to live, we start to take a deeper dive and learn that regardless of our circumstances, our reality can vary depending on how we choose to think. Some people choose to focus on loss, while others choose to embrace the positive events they experience. What we choose to focus on matters. We can mope. We can somewhat enjoy ourselves. Or we can live fully and have the time of our lives. Some of you may have read the last few sentences and felt upset by them because there are times when the stories we tell and hear are so loud, and the emotions we absorb, feel, and hold are so large that it can feel like we don't have a choice when it's time to focus on our thinking. I absolutely have been there and empathize with that conflict. I have learned that it is a false prison. In all three instances, we die because all physical life ends. Still, the experience we create can vary greatly and will determine the quality of that life.

I have not only come to terms with this concept of how to live my life, but I have also fully embraced that our individual reality and life experience are influenced by what we think and how we choose to act on those thoughts. Unfortunately, we will never comprehend all the answers to the great questions in life until we physically die. Until then, we must search and look with our Spirit and remember that life is a game to be enjoyed to the fullest. So when you find yourself thinking and feeling that life is very serious and isn't fun anymore, perhaps it is a sign it is time for you to Unbecome.

Chapter 6

Maslow's Hierarchy of Needs

In 2017, while pregnant with my son Myles, I came across Maslow's Hierarchy of Needs. I remembered it from my Psych 101 class at the University of Hawaii at Manoa. As I read and refreshed my memory, I noticed it mirrored my personal growth journey toward enlightenment and that I could leverage it as a roadmap to help others find their purpose.

To provide a high-level overview for those who find it helpful, Abraham Harold Maslow, born on April 1, 1908, in Brooklyn, New York, was a psychologist and is regarded as the father of humanistic psychology, which digs into positive mental health. He proposed his hierarchy of needs in his 1943 paper "A Theory of Human Motivation" in the journal *Psychological Review*.* [3]

In this paper, Maslow asserts humans have at least five goals or basic needs: physiological, safety, love and belonging, self-esteem, and self-actualization. He illustrates these basic needs in a pyramid model set in order of attainment. We start at the bottom and strive to move

---

[3] Abraham Harold Maslow, "A theory of human motivation". *Psychological Review.* (1943) 50 (4): 370–96, posted August 2000 on Classics in the History of Psychology, psychclassics.yorku.ca/Maslow/motivation.htm.

up the pyramid one need at a time. In order to attain the next level's goal, we only have to satisfactorily meet our needs at the current level. Additionally, we always have access to and can be pulled down to any lower level at any time.

An example of this would be while I'm on the self-esteem level and focusing on career advancement, I suddenly get very sick. My energy and focus would have to transition back to filling my physiological needs. It is absolutely natural to move up and down the chain, ideally driving progress at each level every time you visit it.

To better understand Maslow's model, take a look at the following interpretation of his pyramid. Since we enter this life as newborns at the bottom of the pyramid, we need air, food, water, and clothes. Once that first physiological need is met to our satisfaction, we can then focus on our need for safety and well-being. Next, we focus on our needs for love and belonging, and so on. This process continues up to Maslow's top tier of self-actualization, which refers to the realization of one's full potential. Maslow describes this level as "the desire to accomplish everything that one can, to become the most that one can be" (Maslow 64). I connect this level to discovering and living our life's purpose, which is made possible through our Unbecoming.

Maslow's Hierarchy of Needs

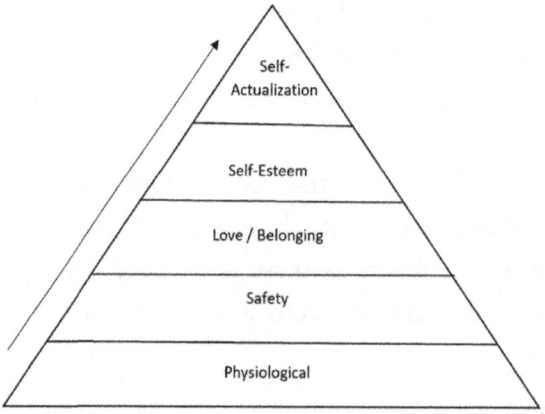

Let's look deeper at an explanation of what is in each hierarchical level by detailing each need more specifically.

Maslow's Hierarchy Levels	Components
Self-Actualization	Morality, Creativity, Spontaneity, Problem-Solving, Lack of Prejudice, Purpose
Esteem	Self-Esteem, Confidence, Career, Achievement, Respect of Others, Respect by Others
Love/Belonging	Friendship, Family, Intimacy
Safety	Security of Body, Employment, Resources, Morality, Family, Health, Property
Physiological	Breathing, Food, Water, Sleep, Shelter, Homeostasis, Excretion

Maslow's pyramid and the following reflection questions will help you identify where you are in your journey towards your purpose, so you know where it may be useful for you to Unbecome.

Reflection Question: Which level are you currently on? Which level takes up most of your energy daily?

More often than we'd like, the level we think we are on and the level we are actually on can be different. The answer to the second question is likely the area you would most want to focus on to help elevate you up the hierarchy.

In our lives, there are many reasons we can find why we are here at this specific point in time. However, of those, one stands apart from the rest. It is your absolute life purpose, the specific reason God created you, and the specific change in the world you were meant to create and share. Per Maslow's Hierarchy of Needs, we must evolve and grow through this pyramid to discover and live out that purpose. In the next chapter, I will bring in some of my own learnings and concepts I have found through my Unbecoming journey to help make Maslow's Hierarchy of Needs even more pragmatic.

Chapter 7

Maslow's Hierarchy and Our Duality

In the figure below, I chart how I see Self-Transformation as a parallel journey to elevating through Maslow's Hierarchy of Needs. The more we practice Unbecoming towards our Spirit Identity, we can transcend towards purpose more effectively. While the pyramid simply shows each level, the process of moving up each level is not clear-cut. The first step is to find which level we are currently in on the pyramid, and then set a goal within that level to fill that need and then access the next level of needs. That's the relatively easy part. The next step is becoming mindful of transforming your subconscious thoughts and beliefs in order to become the being you aspire to be.

Jim Rohn, who I look to as one of my virtual mentors, affirmed this. In his article "The Real Value of Setting Goals," he states:

> *"The real value in setting goals is not in their achievement. The acquisition of the things you want is strictly secondary. The major reason for setting goals is to compel you to become the person it takes to achieve them."*

The objective of any goal is not to achieve the goal itself. Achieving the goal itself is the byproduct of the primary goal. The primary goal is to overcome our own limited, Human selves and activate the unlimited possibility and power of our Spirit selves.

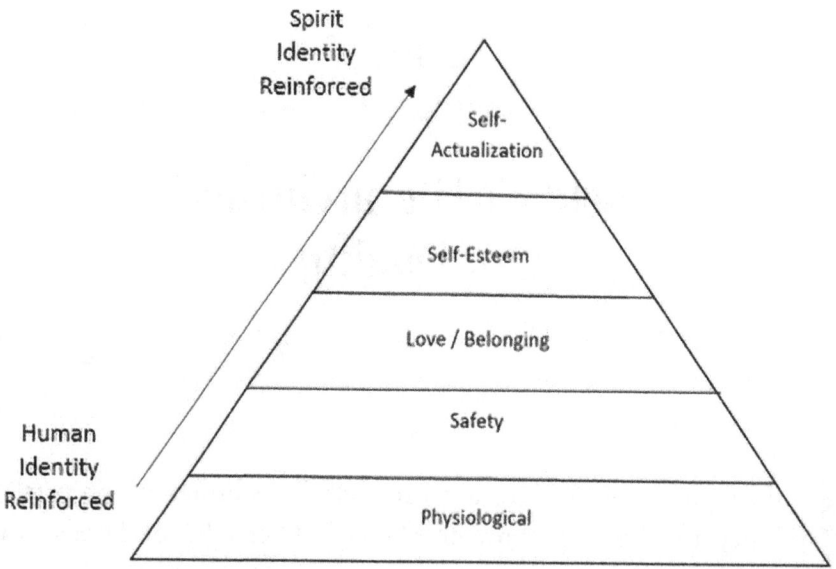

The duality concept I shared in chapter three correlates to Maslow's Hierarchy of Needs in this way and helps us to achieve our goals. And as we elevate up the pyramid, we can choose and be our Spirit selves more consistently.

Human	Maslow's Hierarchy	Spirit
	Self-Actualization & Purpose	Divine, Giving, Faith, Freedom, Intuition, Impact, Holy, Present in the moment, Energy, Living, Awe/Wonder, Holy
Worldly, Getting, Fear, Weighed Down, Five Senses, Finite, Consume, Wants, Pain, Happiness, Perfection, Fixed Mindset, Achievement, Not present, Money	Esteem, Career, & Achievement	Infinite, Create, Needs, Peace, Joy, Progress, Growth Mindset, Healthy
Inauthentic, Lust/Control, Competition, Jealousy, Offense	Love/Belonging	Authentic, Love, Collaboration, Gratitude, Forgiveness,
Insecurity, Adventure	Safety	Security, Safety
Existing, Stimulation, Healthy	Physiological	

This is how I see Maslow's Hierarchy of Needs and my Duality concept working together. Maslow's Hierarchy of Needs is the subconscious process we follow as human beings in this world to improve our tangible quality of life. Once we have an awareness of our Duality, we can consciously choose to Unbecome and be our Spirit self within whatever need or level we are in at the moment, which helps us elevate to Self-Actualization and Purpose.

However, our Unbecoming to our Spirit selves isn't just a linear journey up Maslow's Hierarchy of Needs. There are constant ups and downs within the levels to get to mastery. Think of the trend as very similar to the stock market. There are regular ups and downs, and over a larger span of time, if we are taking action toward our higher self, then there is an overarching upward trend. I believe this is why many who seek self-actualization and purpose recluse. Removing yourself from distractions and temptations makes it easier to elevate and stay in Spirit.

Chapter 8

Religion and Self-Transformation

Many times, this internal physical and spiritual journey can be overwhelming. It helps to have physical support from our family, friends, and coaches. But it is also necessary to have a spiritual support system from God, Jesus, the Holy Spirit, Angels, ArchAngels, and our Ancestors or anything we consider to be within our spiritual realm. This is where I believe religion comes into play. And by religion, I simply mean any trained set of beliefs about how the spiritual world works.

But, before I dig too far, I want to bring back the faith definition I shared in chapter three in the Duality grid. The term faith is often used to refer to a specific religion. I, however, use it to refer to our choice at any given moment to use our brain power to focus on the possibility of a positive future instead of a negative one. I believe faith is often tied to religion because religions generally speak of a promising and abundant future for their believers. I believe you can have faith without religion because, as I've stated above, faith is simply choosing to focus on your desired future state, regardless of your specific beliefs. And our reticular activating system (RAS) enables us to create that desired future because its primary function is to alert the higher brain centers when important messages are received and to filter incoming messages.[4] In other words, our RAS helps us to perceive everything aligned with whatever consumes our focus.

Now, back to religion. I've learned that questioning doctrine and practices is generally frowned upon. Growing up in a strict household, and a Catholic one at that, when asking questions, I often heard the explanation "because I or someone said so" for why I should do things. That logic, or rather illogic, never resonated with me. That reasoning felt controlling and constricting, not empowering and freeing, as Church leaders would exclaim when defining God's love.

To dive deeper into this, let me share with you an experience I had in college. I attended an undergrad Religion course in the Summer of 2002 at the University of Hawaii at Manoa called "Religion and the Meaning of Existence." I greatly appreciated my professor because he provided a safe space to challenge and inquire about traditional religion and spirituality. One example of the hypotheticals he threw out for us to wrangle with was the possibility that humans evolved and created religion as a survival mechanism because those who had hope for a positive future lived a higher quality of life more consistently than those who didn't. This was a fascinating theory to me because it provided a compelling, scientific connection to the value of having a daily, faith-based practice.

Little did I know then that his class gave me a foundation for curiosity and openness as I began my own faith exploration. An additional concept he shared was a distinction between seeing religion as a "spirit" instead of seeing it as an "institution." The "spirit" is the raw, unadulterated nature of the founder of the religion. The "institution" is the organization built by human beings around the founder's nature and spirit that can inadvertently become tainted and tarnished by the human nature of those individuals within the organization.

---

4 "Functions of Reticular Activating System (RAS) | Brain | Neurology," Psychology Discussion, accessed November 1, 2022, https://www.psychologydiscussion.net/brain/functions-of-reticular-activating-system-ras-brain-neurology/2893.

I'll use Christianity as an example of this. Jesus Christ is the Spirit founder of Christianity, which is the institution. Thus, as an institution, it is not surprising that some of the rules or practices are not congruent with Jesus' Teachings or actions. I was intrigued by this concept because it helped me understand the disconnect I sometimes have with religion. This disconnect specifically happens when religions and religious leaders preach or practice things that contradict their beliefs or other principles. Or when there is a lack of understanding of the significance and origin of a tradition that we blindly accept and follow because it is taught to us by our caregivers or mentors when we are young.

As an example of how we mindlessly accept and follow a norm, I've witnessed many religious people, including myself, hesitate to help someone in need, like a homeless person or beggar, because we question their intentions or how they will use what we give them. This is an understandable human tendency, especially in today's society. But is that how Jesus lived? On the contrary, it has always been so profound to me that Jesus chose his Spirit self quickly and consistently in these situations and never hesitated to help others. In fact, he was even criticized by those in His Church for befriending sinners and healing others on the Sabbath. Whenever I feel conflicted about an action or decision, I pray, meditate on it and read scripture and other historical works until I gain enough wisdom and insight into what Jesus did or would do based on how he acted in those situations.

I am very grateful to have had a mentor who encouraged me to discover and experience Jesus' and God's love for myself instead of just taking his or anyone else's words as fact. His invitation and reassurance to explore and deepen my relationship with God encouraged me to embrace my college professor's understanding of religion as institutionalizing someone else's spirit and nature. As a result, I am a proud and devout Christian who belongs to a church. But, I am also mindful to keep my practices and beliefs as true to Jesus' example and nature as much as I can. If an action doesn't fill me with love and peace, I don't do it or find a different way.

Remember that love and peace distinguishes our Spirit selves, whereas pleasure and happiness are of our Human selves. I believe that when a loving and peaceful energy exists, so does God.

Furthermore, I believe the Spiritual realm is One and Universal. Different religions can work together instead of contradicting each other because each is a limited yet valid interpretation of the same expansive, complex experience of life and the meaning of our existence. Whether we are Christian, Muslim, Hindu, Buddhist, or of some other spiritual belief, we are within the same realm that follows the same laws that we are all subject to. So when someone shares a belief that seems surprising or outlandish to me, I am aware that I perceive it this way because it has not been my experience. But that doesn't mean it isn't authentic or possible for the other person. It simply means it hasn't been my perceived reality.

Let me elaborate with this example. Here are three blurbs from three people from entirely different cultures worldwide:

Observer 1

- All kinds of animals, weird creatures, buildings, and machines.
- Very loud, lots of music.
- So many colors.

Observer 2

- Lots and lots of people.
- Happy faces.
- Kids having fun and running around.

Observer 3

- The food looks really tasty.
- Hard to find a place to sit and eat.
- Families enjoying meals together.

If you read them separately without any context to connect them, it can seem as though the three people are in entirely different places. However, what if I revealed to you that each of these three people is at Disneyland and standing within fifteen feet of each other? They do not know each other and do not have a common background. Much like the original tribes scattered across the world, their interpretations of the same experience appear very different. What grabs their attention and how they articulate what hits their senses varies greatly. I think this same dynamic applies to the differences we see in world religions. Still, we are limited in our ability to fully see and articulate the full picture of how the world actually works and came to be.

During an interview with NPR's "Short Wave," behavioral and data scientist Pragya Agarwal examined how unconscious bias affects our thinking. After reviewing her studies, I needed to ask myself to consider this: if we are only able to process about 50 bits of roughly 11 million plus bits of information **per second**, that means **we comprehend less than 0% of what is actually occurring** at any given moment.[5] Knowing this, I have come to understand religion as the interpretation of the spiritual experiences of a collective group of individuals. But if we are only capable of noting 50 bits per second of that Spiritual experience, then individual religions provide only a tiny view of the greater picture. Additionally, keep in mind that each processed bit can be experienced differently by different groups of people, thus providing different interpretations of the same truth. I believe that if we can instead put all the pieces from different vantage points together, we might be able to perceive a clearer, more comprehensive understanding of our God and Universe and the similarities we don't realize we share.

This is the most valuable piece of guidance I can offer - seek an active relationship with God. Do not get this confused with actively seeking a relationship with a religion or a church because institutions are naturally flawed since humans and their nature lead them. It is easy for us as imperfect humans to get distracted and stuck on analyzing, categorizing, judging, and contemplating faith instead of simply PRACTICING it. Seek God - the founder - FIRST in all that you do. For a while and at countless moments, it may feel pointless, confusing, and frustrating. We can get stuck on asking ourselves:

---

5 Emily Kwong, "Understanding Unconscious Bias," NPR, July 15, 2020, https://www.npr.org/2020/07/14/891140598/understanding-unconscious-bias.

- How long will it take to find God?
- Where do we start?
- Who do we reach out to?
- What is the best and fastest way to seek God?
- Will we know Him when we do?

And just like that, you can easily get distracted and stuck thinking about faith instead of just ACTING in faith. With a pure heart and pure intention - for the main, if not sole purpose, of seeking God simply to seek and experience Him rather than for what He can do for you - work to take any step towards a relationship with God. Pull yourself out of lusting for what God can give you and focus on growing in love by loving Him. Each of us has a masterfully crafted and unique life story and purpose. And as a result, we each have a different next step in our journey. Know that God is love, and His love brings peace, joy, and courage. You will learn to know what that love is because the right steps, over time, will result in you having and holding more of it. You will start to see yourself and your life more aligned with your Spirit state as you continue to evolve from your Human one.

I imagine this segment might stir up curiosity, if not some uneasiness, for you and others. And to be completely transparent and share my own vulnerability, my biggest fear is that others might judge or label me as "too Christian" or, ironically, "not Christian enough." Here's what I do know and how I find peace among the different reactions. I could be entirely right about all of this, or I could be wrong. Still, at least I am conscious about what I believe and create in life, rather than subconsciously acting on autopilot from my environmental programming while enduring unnecessary or unwanted suffering. Let's be real: if we understood everything about God and the spiritual realm - that's understanding 100% of 11 million plus bits of information every second - then it probably means that we've passed on and have physically transitioned to the Spirit realm. Until then, let's embrace our Unbecoming and use it as a loving reminder that these are simply snapshots of clarity and wisdom we receive when we allow God to lead us on this journey to be more like Him and share in the chance to help others live fully.

Chapter 9

Taking the First Step

Let's stop and take a moment to review where you are in this process of Unbecoming by going back to Maslow's Hierarchy of Needs. The first step in your self-transformation is identifying where you are in the pyramid. Take a look at which need or needs are the focus of your life right now. Your answer will fall into one of these three categories:

1. Not clear at all.
2. Very clear and obvious.
3. Seemingly very clear and obvious at the superficial level, but unclear once you dig deeper.

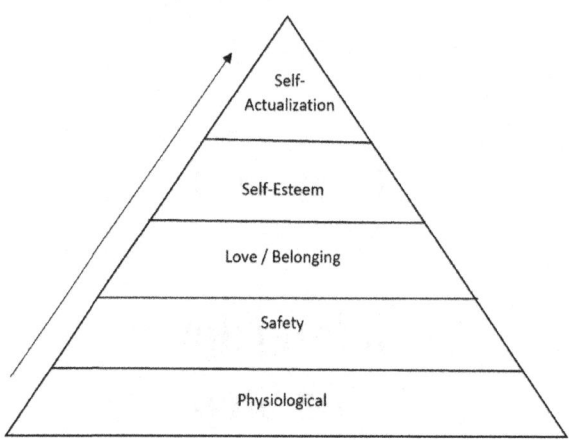

Maslow's Hierarchy of Needs

Regardless of which of these describes your answer, here are some reflection questions that can help you validate which needs are most critical to your transformation at this point in your life.

Reflection Question: What area in your life takes up the most energy or drains your energy and why?

Reflection Question: What aspect of your life do you believe, if improved, would significantly increase your quality of life?

Reflection Question: In which part of your life do you feel "stuck," if any?

These questions will help you conquer the first step, which is knowing where you are. The next chapter will walk you through Steps 2 and 3: figuring out where you want to be (Goal Setting) and how to bridge that gap (Unbecoming).

Chapter 10

Goal Digging

My definition of goal digging is setting, pursuing, and conquering goals over and over again. It is the skill that moves us closer to our dream lives.

"You can't go back and change the beginning, but you can start where you are and change the ending."

-C.S. Lewis

Unbecoming is a tactic you can employ to evolve, grow and reach your goals. Setting a goal is the first step. Knowing exactly where you are going is critical to achieving anything. There are many goal-setting models out there. The most powerful insights I've had in using various models over the years are that:

1. Authenticity, reinforcement, and evolution of the WHY behind any goal are critical in getting us to take and STAY in ACTION;
2. Being extremely detailed helps build clarity for each next best ACTION.

Note how both insights are tied to ACTION: shifting our dreaming into doing and our thinking into being out of our heads and into the world.

Here are five questions I recommend answering when setting a goal and creating an action plan. Write down the most accurate and to-the-point answers you can think of for them. If you find that it takes time to gain clarity on any answer, that's a perfect signal that you are digging deep enough to answer authentically. If you're still feeling unclear after giving yourself some time to respond, stop thinking. Take the plan you have so far and implement it. While implementing your plan, pay attention to how you feel and the thoughts you have. If you're feeling positive and are gaining momentum, then you're on the right track. If not, consider your lessons, insights, and observations from taking ACTION and see if those help you adjust or finetune your plan or goal.

- **What** do I want to achieve or create?
  Be as specific as possible because the details help our brains know what solutions and clues to look for and focus on. For example, "I want to run faster" is too vague. "I want to run one mile in under five minutes" is more specific.
- **When** do I need to achieve or create my goal?
  Set a date. If we do not provide our brains with a date, there is a greater likelihood we will procrastinate or deprioritize taking action.
- **Why** is it necessary that I create this goal? What will it mean for me if I don't achieve it? Remember, your authentic WHY is usually masked by logical reasons. For example, "I want to lose weight to feel good and be healthy." That's a good reason. However, the more accurate and authentic reason may be, "I want to lose weight because I'm sick and tired of being called fat and feeling ugly." This may not sound as politically correct as the first one, but it identifies the greater Human need you may have for self-confidence and esteem over health and will help you attain your goal better.

- **Who** do I need to partner with to create and achieve this goal? Partners can be both those that can help us or benefit from our work.
- **How** do I achieve or create this goal?
    - Step 1 - List all the steps you can think of for completing your goal.
    - Step 2 - Look at any significant steps and break them down into smaller steps, if possible. For example: "Go to the gym five times a week" could be broken down into "Get a gym membership" and "Go to the gym two times a week to start."
    - Step 3 - Put them in order if you still need to do so. This will be your plan.

Don't be concerned if you want to go back and finetune your responses to these questions. You can do this at any time. After all, you'll soon discover that setting goals is not a one-time deal. You may decide that you'll need to dig further. For example, I've found that when answering any goal I want to set for myself, I have actually come to witness and believe that my brain has the power to access any answer I want in the universe IF I program and command it to seek that answer out. The details we give our brains help them subconsciously "see" clues we normally miss. And since we are no longer missing them, we will work more to incorporate them into our goals.

An additional example is when I answer why it is essential for me to create this goal. In writing the answer to this question, I realized that for me, authentic WHYs were emotionally charged. The more emotionally charged, the better. This is because, as humans, we act when there is emotion. Consider this: any significant action we have ever taken in life was usually because of an emotional event - whether good or bad. Having an emotionally powerful and clear "why and why not" allows us to not only tap into our primitive programming for our needs and survival but also use this principle to our advantage. We take that principle and intentionally assign big, positive emotions to achieve our goal so that a reward is attached to that new, desired behavior. Consequently, we also assign a big, negative emotion to not achieving our goal, thereby attaching a threat to that old, undesired behavior. As a result, you are training your brain to move towards the reward and away from the threat you have selected.

Another reason an authentic and powerful WHY is necessary for goal conquering is when we first create new programming and habits, we come to realize that our prior programming and habits have an incredibly strong hold on us. They can get in the way of progress. At the same time, life continues to happen, and different challenges will come and possibly distract us from our goals. There will be multiple times when the strength and emotional value of our authentic WHY will be the only thing that is able to get us through these challenges. If we say it differently, the meaning of our "it" has to be so great that when we feel like giving up and have every logical reason to do so, we remember what we will gain (reward) and give to the world by accomplishing our goal and what we will lose (threat) if we fail to take action. Consequently, that authentic WHY will be so powerful and meaningful that it will enable us to activate and stay in our Spirit while continuing to take ACTION.

Imagine it this way. Picture yourself feeling exhausted and sleeping in your warm, comfortable bed. What could you want so badly that you would immediately jump up and do the thing you're supposed to do without hesitation? If you have an answer for that, TERRIFIC - use that! If you don't, the homework for you is to go and find what that WHY is for you. Know this - we all have an authentic WHY that is extremely powerful. We just have to put in the work to self-discover it.

Answering these questions will not be easy. Many will see challenges as signs that there is something wrong with our goal. That can absolutely be true in some cases. However, more often than not, challenges are one way our universe helps us to clarify what we want and why we want it. Rather than thinking the universe is working against us, choose to see that the universe is on our side, helping us along.

Let me repeat that in case it helps ground us more in this truth: CHOOSE to see that the universe is ON YOUR SIDE, helping you along.

Whenever I encounter a notable barrier towards a goal or an action that is scary or uncertain because it's new and pushes me out of my comfort zone, I see that barrier or challenge as God's way of asking me, "Are you certain you want this? How badly do you want this?" If my answers are "Yes" and "Enough to overcome anything that gets in my way," then I push forward no matter what. I stay in ACTION. If my answers are "No" because "I'm not sure or don't want it badly enough," then I: (1) work on identifying the lessons or "aha" moments God has intentionally sent me to discover through that process and gain more clarity on my true WHAT and WHY; (2) modify my goal; and (3) make a plan.

Let's continue to dive deeper into these challenges. Here are some reflection questions that will help you to proactively troubleshoot barriers or stumbling blocks:

Reflection Question: Barriers - What potential barriers do I see getting in the way of my taking action on any of the "how" steps above? Remember to adjust or include another Action to account for that barrier. For example, Barrier: "I'm not sure when I'll be able to get a gym membership." Solution: "Get a gym membership on Monday at 4 pm after work." Remember, pick a date and time because we are more likely to follow through on an action when we schedule it.

Reflection Question: Reality Check - Am I willing to do what it takes and make the necessary trade-offs to achieve this goal or create this precisely as I have written it? If not, then adjust the goal until the answer to this question is yes.

I find this reality check is crucial because it keeps us accountable by ensuring we are willing and able to do what it takes to conquer a goal. If we find that we aren't willing or able to take action, it doesn't mean you can't or won't reach that goal. It just means the path to get there may now have to be different from what we initially planned. It may seemingly take longer or take more steps, but you can find just as much joy and excitement by living through the journey as you will in discovering the destination.

Here's an example. I want to get promoted to the next level leadership role in my company, but I don't want to relocate or am unable to relocate for that position. This doesn't mean that I'm not capable of performing at the next level or won't ever get there. It just means I might have to wait until a local opportunity comes up and, in the meantime, find different ways to show the value I can add to that next level.

We need to remember setting a goal is primarily about becoming, not getting or attaining. So while our Why for a goal can be powerful, sometimes it is so transformative that we must be willing to identify and address our current mindset or programming that serves our current, not future, identity.

Reflection Question: Limiting Mindset or Programming - What limiting beliefs do I have about myself or my situation that will get in the way of me taking and staying in Action? After all, mindset or belief drives every action we take. Usually, when we make goals, we put most of our energy and reflection on the Action, as we discussed earlier in this chapter. But we can't forget to also focus on the mindset or programming that exists in our current habits to better understand how to achieve our newly desired ones. Consider the Current State/Desired State scenario on the next page.

	Current State	**Desired State**
Outcome	I feel tired in the morning and want to sleep in.	I want to feel amazing in the morning and feel like I can conquer the world!
Action	Get 4-6 hours of sleep at night. Go to bed whenever I'm done watching TV and browsing my social media accounts.	Get 8 hours of sleep at night. Go to bed by 10 pm during the week and watch TV shows and surf social media only on the weekends.
Belief/ Identity	I am a fan of my TV show. I care more about staying caught up with my TV show and what's on social media than I do my well-being.	I am well-rested. Being well-rested is a top priority because it helps me be my best and have a productive day at work and home.

Note: We'll see this grid again in the "Love and Belonging" chapter, where we dig more into Belief and Identity and how we can leverage that to move us toward our desired state.

Even with all this work, life can interject, and sometimes the plan must change. For example, while pursuing the next level at your job, someone buys your company, and now that job or both jobs are lost. Or, no matter how hard you try to make it work, you finally realize that you have to break out of a toxic relationship in order to keep yourself whole. Even when circumstances change, learn to adjust and use those changes as a first step because only then will you be open to the next ones. Understanding our authentic WHY and moving progressively forward will keep you on the path to your goal.

Goal Digging Reminder - Remember to Set a Goal for Who We Might Become.

We can forget that setting a goal is primarily about becoming, not getting or attaining. How would you behave if you knew you couldn't fail? How would you act if, no matter how things turned out, you knew that God has a way of making it work out for your own good or even better than you had thought for yourself? How would you behave if you knew you could live the life you want because God is both with and in you?

Here's the great news - you can! Naturally, your Human side is kicking in and has already thought of the twelve reasons why you think you can't. After all, everyone wants to be Oprah, Beyonce, or Warren Buffet. But not everyone is willing to DO the WORK and TAKE the RISKS needed to BE Oprah, Beyonce, or Warren Buffet. It's not because you can't. It's because it's hard to change. It's because the comfort and certainty your current situation gives you make you feel safe, and our Human side craves safety. Often, certainty and comfort have a stronger pull on us than our big and powerful dream because our Human side is programmed for safety and survival. But, ask yourself again: is there anything you want so badly that you would find a way to do it no matter what barriers come your way? Use THAT to drive you. If it helps, find your role model. Do what they did to get there. If you don't do it respectfully, you don't want it bad enough.

Realize that you are the only thing stopping you.

-Unknown

Chapter 11

Physiological

I would like to share some insights I have learned about my own body and physiological well-being. By encouraging each of us to know about our physical selves, the magnificent biology of our bodies, and their innate, miraculous ability to heal, you can better understand what practices might work best for you.

Today, when we say someone is healthy, we often mean that the person is without disease. The word health has origins related to the word whole, which according to Oxford Languages, is defined as "a thing that is complete in itself." From that, my understanding of being healthy is being able to heal myself of any foreign object, substance, or force that my body may negatively interact with so that I can be whole and complete again.

Most of us have seen those memes or posts online about the cycle of life. When we are babies, we are helpless and need our parents to care for us. As we grow up, we learn to be independent and take care of ourselves. Then as we become elderly, we return to that helpless, child-like state where we rely on others again. This "helpless" categorization makes this state seem unappealing; we are anxious to be able to grow older and do more. However, I have come to believe that our baby state is our optimal physical state, as well as our Spiritual state. During this time, we are masters of our being. There is no fear of taking action to grow because there is nothing yet to unlearn. We are content with Being because there are no expectations imposed on us. Thus, there is no need to "Become" or "Unbecome."

Let's take a look at this a bit further. Healthy newborns are born: 1) breathing from their diaphragm, 2) flexible, 3) drinking fluids throughout the day, 4) getting sufficient sleep, 5) processing food and expelling waste after almost every meal, and 6) enjoying Being while not being preoccupied or stressed.

How much have we moved away from our child-like state? Let's explore this together.

In the following grid, assess how you are feeling and whether or not you are in a Newborn State. If you aren't, try the potential healing activities. Also, consider partnering with your medical doctor, naturopathic doctor, therapist, and other experts to understand how to return your body to these optimal states.

Newborn State	Your Current State? Y/N	Potential Healing Activity
Breathing from Diaphragm		Daily belly breathing exercise
Flexibility		Yoga, stretching, weekly chiropractor visits, monthly massage appointment
Fluids throughout the day		Half to one ounce of water per pound of weight daily, a bit of sea salt in water as an electrolyte[6]
Getting sufficient sleep		7-9 hours a day, practice 4-7-8 breathing at bedtime[7]
Processing food/expelling waste after each meal		High nutrient and whole/unprocessed foods when able, 5 servings of fruits & vegetables daily (smoothies), intermittent fasting, minimize animal meat or products, regular prebiotics and probiotics, detoxes/cleanses
Enjoying being and not preoccupied/stress		Meditation, therapy, coaching, motivational videos and/or songs, affirmations, limiting distractions, focus on things that bring you joy, moderate to strenuous physical activity while listening to slow-paced music, exploring nature, acupuncture, sound healing, herbs and supplements (check with a Naturopathic Doctor)

I know we can't ever fully bring our physiology back to the Newborn State. But the recommendations above are just a few of the many ways to optimize our physiology and protect our bodies' innate ability to heal themselves. Food and gut health has been a big focus for me, so let's dig into that part of my Unbecoming journey first.

---

6 Karthik Kumar, MBBS, "How Much Water Should You Drink Based on Your Weight?" MedicineNet, medically reviewed on February 1, 2023, https://www.medicinenet.com/How_much_water_to_drink_based_on_your_weight/article.htm.

7 "How To Do the 4-7-8 Breathing Exercise," Cleveland Clinic, September 6, 2022, https://health.clevelandclinic.org/4-7-8-breathing/.

While I am relatively healthy, I still have a lot of room to grow in the above areas. The most challenging shifts for me have been the last two, given the learned habits I grew up with around food and work. I am Filipino and grew up in Hawaii. Filipino and Hawaiian cultures are big foodie cultures. Variation is absolutely present in many of our meals. Moderation is not. While fresh fruits and vegetables are a large part of these cuisines, most Filipino and Hawaiian eateries focus on heaping piles of delicious and tasty carbs and meats. Additionally, canned goods, specifically Vienna sausage, corned beef, sardines, and SPAM, were a regular part of my diet growing up.

Learning how my body worked and reconditioning its processes became a big focus for me when I was pregnant. However, despite my being categorized as "healthy" pre-pregnancy, I became a gestational diabetic during both pregnancies. Fortunately, I was able to control it via diet and monitoring my blood sugar throughout the day. My OBGYN reassured me that this was common and that I shouldn't worry about it since I could control my sugar levels without medication and that they would likely go back to normal postpartum (which they did, thank God). Even with her reassurance, I was still very curious about why I became a gestational diabetic and understanding how it indicates that I might be predisposed to Type 2 diabetes later in life. Armed with insights from my doctors and dietician, as well as my own research, I learned what I ate, when I ate, and even HOW I ate (fast, slow, etc.) mattered to my digestion. Just like any other machine or vehicle, there are certain kinds of things that you can put in it that are better for short-term performance and long-term maintenance.

In working to improve my eating habits, I learned that I ate almost always for pleasure instead of performance. When I made that discovery and began to see that my body could be a powerful tool - my vehicle to do work in this world - it became easier for me to intentionally choose healthier foods and eating habits because of my desire to perform better each time. Additionally, I have been even more mindful of how the food I eat impacts the amount and quality of my energy since that energy gets transferred to me. As a result, there are days I am intentionally vegetarian in order to allow my body a chance to reset and renew my internal energy.

Speaking of performance, I have learned to be obsessed with high performance. While that is not necessarily a negative thing in and of itself, the risk I found with focusing on performance is that it reinforced the false goal of perfection versus progress. The underlying learned narrative that I must strive for perfection and be able to do everything well was at the core of my preoccupation and stress. I was trying to be phenomenal with my work and projects while also being a world-class wife, coordinating day-to-day activities for the home and kids, making time for family and friends, and more. I put so much pressure on myself to be everything; I forgot to just BE. I withdrew from the current moment and existed in the past or future. No wonder it was so easy to feel overwhelmed and exhausted. I was trying to be in two or three places at one time in my head. All that did was rob me of the moment while the cycle perpetuated. I've always known that "Tomorrow isn't promised." I'm sadly and soberly reminded of that fact anytime someone in my tribe passes away. Yet, even though I knew it, it was easy to fall into the trap of living for tomorrow instead of today.

Health is everything. Being subject to the Human condition is problematic in itself. A healthy body allows for an easier connection to your Spirit self. It is very common in this life, especially when you are young and feel like you still have your whole life ahead of you, to push your body to the limit and not take care of it. We have to remember that we are living beings. What you put in consistently matters. What doesn't come out and stays in matters. A day here or there of not taking care of yourself may not make a big difference. But, no matter what happens in life, be sure to create disciplined practices around your health because what you feel and hold inside impacts what you're able to put out.

Chapter 12

Financial Safety

Poor, Rich, Wealthy

Most people in the world fall under the Poor and Rich categories. Improving your finances isn't directly about getting or acquiring money. It's about becoming a person who is worthy and capable of creating and attracting those resources, opportunities, relationships, and wealth. So, to start this section, I first want to share my definitions of Poor, Rich, and Wealthy as a foundation for how money and mindset are connected.

- Poor = Net negative money & money is the Master
- Rich = Net positive money & money is still the Master
- Wealthy = Net positive money & you are the Master

My dream for everyone in this world, and especially you reading this book, is that you will be able to achieve the mindset and belief system of a wealthy person so that you can act and be wealthy.

My First Transformation

My first significant transformation with my finances began in 2008 when I was at my lowest point in life. Just as a reminder of the financial component of my situation mentioned earlier in this book, I was about $35,000 in debt and earning little money as a pharmacy technician, with aspirations to become a pharmacist. I was not aware of the stronghold money had come to have on me. I had spent money until the debt was large enough and past due enough. The anxiety and stress I felt from just thinking about getting calls and letters from collection agencies regarding delinquent accounts, let alone actually getting and dodging those calls and letters, overwhelmed me. There were times the weight was so heavy it was easy to find ways to escape its reality. However, I knew I had to make a change if I wanted a different reality. This transformation was grueling, but I am so grateful for the wisdom and power I gained, having had to overcome it.

At the core of my financial blunder was an unhealthy relationship with money that stemmed from an inaccurate understanding of its nature and utility. First, it took a lot of reflection and courage for me to see and own the fact that I idolized money. I know some of you may think it's extreme to use the word idolize when describing my relationship with money since, generally, it's used with respect for gods. Plus, it's uncomfortable to think we could be so shallow as to worship money. But, consider this: how much time and energy would you say you spend on an average week or month thinking about money, making money, considering how much money you have, whether you will have enough, and how you will get more? Now, how much time do you spend in that same week or month thinking about God, spending time with God, and reflecting on your relationship with God, and when you'll get more time with God? Lastly, which do you spend more time on?

We give money incredible power in this world. So much so that it is one of the top reasons people get divorced. One day, I had an epiphany that since humans created money as a tool, we are its master. Yet, somehow we've reversed that power dynamic and let money rule us. My pastor asserted, "Money falsely promises to provide what only God can - security, worth, confidence, happiness, relationships." However, we seem to pursue money more than we pursue God.

During this low period in my life, I wasn't where I thought I'd be or where I wanted to be in life. I looked to money and the things it could get me to make me feel better about myself and my situation. It was a denial mechanism for me. I subconsciously thought if I didn't have the career or relationship I wanted, at least it could look like I had it all together. I bought into this idea that I could hide behind the brand names and lavish outings, and no one would see that I was struggling and lost.

In a quiet moment, I saw I was leaning on money to provide the things only God can. It was during this time that I made the choice to draw closer to God. Part of my strategy for getting out of debt was to lean on God to fill me up so that I wouldn't need to rely on money to do that anymore. It was incredibly empowering to take back control and free myself from being a slave to money. I googled templates and best practices for personal budgets, made a budget, and stuck to it. I made the decision from that point on that I was going to remain the master; I would tell my money where to go.

The second key action in my economic transformation was to face my debt. I pulled out all the letters I had piled up, contacted each credit card company, and calculated my total debt. While the $35,000 was defeating, I felt a sense of empowerment by simply knowing what it was. I listened to Suze Orman frequently during this time. The stories and insights she shared in her videos and shows made me feel more and more confident that I could pay off all my debt. She also taught me how to know if you can or cannot afford something.

Additionally, I paired up with a credit consolidation company to help work with the credit card companies to bring down my debt and combine them into one amount with a lower interest rate. Seeing one set amount, albeit larger, to pay off instead of eight different amounts with the same total made it feel less daunting. I learned it is always easier to tackle something when you know what you're up against. Something in that specificity enables your brain to figure out solutions that are hard to see when the problem or issue is vague.

I also realized my dodging collection calls wasn't simply because I didn't have the money. It was mainly because I was incredibly embarrassed and didn't know how I would get the money to pay it all off. Later, I had to look deeper and realize that not calling the agents wasn't because I couldn't face them. It was that acknowledging them and having those conversations would make me have to own my role in this mess I was in. I didn't want to admit that I was the one to blame, and I did everything I could to avoid that self-confrontation.

The third thing I did was find ways to make additional income. At that time, I was pretty smart but lacked clarity in my gifts and abilities. I knew I had strong people skills, so I sought out jobs where that was valuable. In addition to being a pharmacy technician, I got a job as a bartender a couple nights during the week. And a good friend helped me get a job as a waitress during the other nights. (I am forever grateful for her because I made some great tips from that gig.) This was all while taking post-graduate classes to bring my GPA back up again. Man, did I hustle during that time. Thank God I had all that energy back then. The combination of spending less and making more helped me pay off ALL of my $35,000 debt in under two years.

Lastly, I want to talk about passive income streams, which are ways to earn money with little to no work. I didn't employ this tactic at the time because I didn't know much about it then. But my husband and I have been more intentional about it, and it has been a game changer for us. Passive income enables us to mentally break free from the stronghold money has on us as human beings. It empowers us to stay true to our purpose and values and act accordingly. Even more meaningful, leveraging passive income allows us to better protect and invest the currency that matters most - time.

I shared near the beginning of this book that we are a product of our environment. Therefore, we must be mindful of our environment and change it if it is not serving our Spirit. I know so many people who stay in a work environment that isn't productive for them emotionally, mentally, spiritually, or even physically. Yet, they stay because they really like the money the job pays. We generally spend more time in our work environment than in any other place. So how we feel about that environment makes a big difference in our quality of life. We should be aware that the paycheck we get isn't worth the toxicity a poor work environment can cause within us. Having even one substantive passive stream of income puts you in a better position to FREELY CHOOSE your environment, as well as the kind of work you do daily for active income. To start, it's good to have one stream of passive income. Later, you can expand to multiple. If you choose, you can even create a life where all your income is passive.

Again, having income other than your W2 gives you the power and freedom to dictate what you do with your time on this earth. There are more ways than ever to generate passive income. Here are several that have become popular:

- Real Estate - rental property, rent space in your home, crowd-funding, multifamily
- Stocks
- Cryptocurrency
- Loan Money to People or Businesses
- Referral Marketing
- Write a Blog or Book :)
- Create a Podcast
- Cash Back Apps
- Display Ads
- Sponsored Posts
- Create Educational Content

Order of Spending

The order of spending matters because it reflects what you value as more or less important. In America, there is a general tendency to spend money in this order - lifestyle, bills, savings (if any is left), and donations (again, if there is anything left to give). To spend money in the Spirit state would be to do the exact reverse. Give FIRST. Then SAVE. Or think of this concept differently: invest in your future self or your future endeavors, such as saving to open a business or attend a seminar. Next, pay your bills and debt. Lastly, use what's left toward your lifestyle. Living over our means is an unfortunate phenomenon in America. We must learn to live under our means in order to truly succeed.

Give Generously

I'm calling out this concept separately because it's that important. In mastering my money, I learned that the most powerful thing we can do is to not invest but give GENEROUSLY of what we have. And give FIRST.

There are a few critical beliefs that this practice uses to help reprogram our brains to give when done intentionally and consistently:

1. Gratitude - a humble acknowledgment that all our blessings come from God.
2. Abundance mindset - which is part of the Spirit state. The person who does not give has a belief that he/she does not have enough. The person who gives has a belief of more than enough.
3. Giving unlocks blessings because we can only receive what we offer or put out. Think of this as a cycle of energy or karma.

Challenge yourself to give generously and watch your quality of life in both the Human/physical and Spiritual/energy realms multiply. A practice that has helped me stay disciplined about giving is increasing it by at least 1% of my total income every year.

Tithing

One way to give generously is tithing. Tithing was always an odd concept for me. I felt it carried a connotation of pressure and obligation. You could almost imagine people saying, "You have to give every week" or "Don't be that person who doesn't give." Or even "A pure desire to give is an act of love for another person ." At times, it also felt fearful that you were somehow going against the Bible if you did not tithe. At church on Sundays during collection time, I thought giving $1 was a big deal, and the people who gave $5 or $10 were generous. Anyone who gave more than that was out of their mind. I hesitated giving more to the Church on Sundays because: 1) I didn't think they needed the money, and 2) I didn't fully trust where the money was going. But later, I began to embrace tithing when I thought of it as disciplined giving. My Church in Massachusetts helped me make that change. They showed me there are churches out there that are intentionally transparent with where they spend the funds they receive.

So, if you aren't currently with a church you trust or know where your funds are going, ask for a summary or find a church you can trust. If you're the latter and are working on finding a new church home, don't let that be an excuse to not give. I believe you don't have to give to a physical church. Give to a cause that helps people, give with love, and be disciplined with your giving. I give the most significant part of our family's tithe to our Church. Still, I also tithe to organizations I believe do God's work, even if they are not labeled as Christian or religious.

An additional way I give is whenever I see an opportunity of need, and I am moved to do so. Examples of this would be paying for a fellow patron's meal or blessing someone on the side of the street who is asking for help. I used to be hesitant to give this way. The Human in me would talk myself into why I shouldn't give. "Oh, they will use it to buy drugs or alcohol." "They don't even look like they are in need. They have decent clothes and don't look homeless." I've learned to overcome those earthly, self-serving thoughts and give from my heart instead of my head. It has done wonders in allowing me to grow and be even more loving and like God.

For me, the discipline and routine of giving are the difference between random acts of generosity and tithing. It is a powerful practice to give regularly. Again, like I mentioned in the "Give Generously" portion of this section, I encourage you, and even dare you, to do this **weekly for one year** and see what personal growth, insights, and blessings it unlocks for you.

So how much should we tithe weekly? The Bible says 10% of our income. However, my pastor opened my eyes to a different way of seeing it. Maybe the Bible literally meant 10%. Or perhaps the Bible could also be saying 10% symbolically. A double-digit number, like 10%, is significant enough to make us uncomfortable. Giving loose change or a few dollars is relatively easy every now and then. But giving an amount that causes you to pause and to choose to do so intentionally while knowing that this sacrifice impacts what you do because you are giving resources away is not easy. That is why tithing is a wonderful mechanism for the transformation of both your heart and mind.

To help you with this transformation, try using this as your guide. Give a dollar amount weekly that challenges your heart; that triggers the Human condition of greed in you. How do you find that amount, you ask? Ask yourself this question:

What would cause you to raise your hand and pay without any hesitation on a fairly regular basis?

I was in my late twenties when I did this reflection, and my answer was, "When having a girls' night out with friends, I do not hesitate to pay for a round of shots. In fact, I'm ecstatic about it. Yet, when I think of taking that same $100 and giving it to someone in need, I think twice about doing so." I didn't spend much time dissecting why there was that disconnect for me. I just knew that it didn't logically make sense, and I didn't want that to be the condition of my heart. So that week, I started tithing $100 weekly. I automated my tithing with autopay to ensure it went through. Automating also allowed me to use that energy on how I should best direct the rest of my money. And when it became a routine and didn't sting anymore to give this amount, I celebrated and gave thanks for the growth I had achieved. I even found the desire to increase it came without any hesitations. As I mentioned above, there came a point where I could easily calculate the amount as a percent of my income. That calculation is what I continue to use now when increasing my tithing by at least 1% every year.

If you're reading this and feel you don't have enough to give, I want to respectfully remind you that that is just a feeling. Give whatever amount truly challenges your heart. You'll know you feel challenged because you will hesitate to give that amount and feel uneasy. The fear of not having enough will come up inside of you. If a dollar or a penny makes you feel uneasy or uncertain, then a dollar or a penny is a meaningful start. Tithing is about conditioning our hearts towards generosity, which is Spirit, rather than survival, which is Human. Additionally, if you own a business, I urge you to apply this same tithing and disciplined giving model to your P&L statements and strategic planning: give first, routinely, and increasingly to others with the first fruits of your labor. This practice should transcend us as individuals and encourage us to share our good fortunes with others.

Too Much Money

Is there such a thing as having "too much money?" I have an absolute financial freedom dollar amount, which is what you need to pay for your dream lifestyle. And according to Tony Robbins' *Money: Master the Game*, you should have one also. As I've worked on my plan to achieve that amount, I've come to reflect on whether I need that money all at once or in smaller amounts repeatedly over my lifetime. I think many are like me and think if I had X amount of money right now, I'd be set forever. But I've begun to wonder if it even works that way.

I think of the story in Exodus 16 - "Manna and Quail from Heaven." In this story, the Israelites were about thirty days into their journey from Egypt to the Promised Land. They were hungry (and possibly hangry) and complained about being out in the wilderness, even wishing they had died or still been enslaved back in Egypt. Being fed seemed better than being free in that difficult moment. So God showed grace and provided manna and quail to eat. But he directed them to only gather enough for that day and to not save any, for there would be a fresh supply the next day. Some did not listen to His instructions and were disappointed to see their saved food rotten and full of maggots when they woke up. As a result, they learned to trust His direction and only gather what they needed for each day.

This story made me consider how the world has trained us to believe we must hoard or stockpile rather than trust God to supply our needs daily. I'm not saying you don't need to save some of your money. I think we should each have a minimum of six to nine months worth of savings. Frankly, having learned from the COVID pandemic, I would now stretch that to twelve months. But how much more do we really need after that? Do I really need to acquire money forever, or is there a sensible point where I can have enough for certain moments in time, then reallocate the remaining funds and energy I use towards good works or creating experiences for myself and my family? Maybe it makes sense to turn down the more demanding, higher-paying job and to say "yes" to the lower-paying job that allows me time to do the things that bring me joy. Perhaps my absolute financial freedom number can be less than it is right now, so I can attain financial freedom sooner than I think.

The Most Valuable Currency of All

There are two kinds of currency that matter spiritually, and neither is money. They are time and energy. We are given a certain amount when we are born, and it decreases until it is depleted when we die. Energy is dynamic and renewable: we can change its quantity and quality moment by moment. It is the life force within us. Time and energy have significantly more value than money. Most people aren't able to truly comprehend this fully. They have time and energy without money and are not content when they should be overjoyed. Money means nothing when you don't have time and energy. So, invest in your personal time and energy, and be intentional about where you spend them.

Abundance vs. Scarcity

By nature, our Human state begets all things human. Thus, our Spirit state begets all things spirit. If we are in the latter state, our authentic selves are both engaged and magnetic and help our spirits attract abundance and overflow of resources, both intangible and tangible. Meanwhile, our inauthentic selves do not. When I think of being able to attract resources and have an abundant mindset, I literally envision myself as if I were telekinetic or psychokinetic. I imagine myself standing outside in my yard with my arms outstretched, actively trying to pull and draw money or resources towards me from far away. That concept seems nearly impossible! And it's highly inaccurate. Even if telekinesis or psychokinesis do exist, it won't work like that for me because I don't have either ability. However, when we are focused on being our Spirit selves, and all those identities on the left side of the duality chart place us in our natural, flawless child-like state, by definition, we are magnetic and have abundance. So money and resources are already drawn to us because of the energy we release and emit into the universe through our thoughts, words, emotions, moods, actions, and even the things we consume and hold within our bodies.

But we must be careful when we encounter actions and events in the physical realm that trigger our Human need for survival. By allowing ourselves to be triggered in that way restricts us within our Human selves and impedes our magnetic ability. This is where we lack abundance and live in a place of scarcity. Consider it this way. Think of our Human selves as a full-body suit. When we wear that suit, there is a barrier that protects us from the physical world and its dangers. Consequently, this barrier can also keep out all the good that wants to get through to us.

I used to think that the resources I needed to reach all my goals were miles away from me. I've since learned that they are not that far away at all. The abundance of anything is right on the outside of our energy periphery. When we can be brave, to Unbecome and shed our Human facades so that we can be our Spirit selves, we no longer have anything blocking that abundance. We are free and open to receive everything God desires to bless us with.

Chapter 13

Love and Belonging

I don't know everything there is to know about love, but I have come to understand what it is to me and, perhaps more importantly, what it is not. In the "Our Duality" chapter, I create a distinction between Love and Lust/Control, with Love being a part of the Spirit state and Lust/Control of the Human state. Often when we think of love and lust, we generally think of intimate or romantic relationships and categorize them as such throughout the majority of those unions.

I think love and lust can be used to describe all relationships, regardless of the context. Furthermore, the relationship is most accurately categorized by data from multiple series of interactions rather than the current or desired feeling from the relationship. For example, most married couples would describe their relationships as love, even though most are likely based on lust.

For me, love is not a feeling. It is ACTION. I want to unpack this more since understanding the difference between the two has transformed the quality of my relationships. **Love is ACTION towards another being that is aligned with our Spirit nature.** It is all the traits in the left-hand column in the Duality grid. Love is a divine action rooted in our authentic self, focused on giving, service, gratitude, and forgiveness, and results in joy and peace for all. Lust is the opposite. It is an action towards another being that is aligned with our Human nature and represents all the traits in the right-hand column. Lust is focused on getting, self-preserving, and having control, easily offended and influenced by external factors that are highly sensationalized and emotional.

> "If you want to know someone's mind, listen to their words. If you want to know their heart, watch their actions."
>
> -Helen Barry

1 Corinthians 13:4-7 (NIV) speaks of this same concept. "Love is patient, love is kind. It does not envy, it does not boast, it is not proud. It does not dishonor others, it is not self-seeking, it is not easily angered, it keeps no record of wrongs. Love does not delight in evil but rejoices with the truth. It always protects, always trusts, always hopes, always perseveres."

Most people in meaningful, romantic relationships would say they are in a love relationship. Most people in platonic relationships also say they are in a love relationship, not a lustful one. I propose that whether or not a relationship is categorized as love or lust depends fully and solely on the actions each person is bringing into the relationship. There can be marriages that are lustful because lust isn't just about being physically intimate. It's about focusing on what you get from the relationship or how it benefits you. Work relationships can be based on love because love isn't just about being emotionally intimate. It's about focusing on what you can give in that relationship or how you can help the person in that relationship with you benefit and thrive. I like this definition of love because it's comprehensive: it articulates what love is and what it isn't. It reminds us that relationships take work, and it is the work we put in most consistently that dictates the kind of relationship it is. Now, it's absolutely healthy for a relationship to have both lust and love because we are both Human and Spirit. However, what I want to bring awareness to is that when a relationship has pain or tension, it's because lust is the greater dynamic at play, not love. Understanding this difference is empowering and encouraging because it asserts we can change the quality of any relationship moment by moment.

> *"When you like a flower, you just pluck it. But when you love a flower, you water it daily."*
>
> *-Buddha*

For all relationships, especially when you are a leader in the relationship, give more words of encouragement instead of advice. It does so much more for one's Spirit and the relationship. Our job in a relationship isn't to judge or criticize. It is to help our loved ones feel valued and capable of their greatness so they remain in faith, hope, and love.

The Power of Love

In 2019, I participated in Tony Robbins' Leadership Academy. During this event, volunteers from the audience were invited to join in coaching activities. I was incredibly moved by one in particular.

All attendees were put into teams for the entire conference. After our Master Coach had asked for a volunteer to come on stage, one of the teams immediately roared to get his attention. In fact, this team of about ten participants was so loud they captured everyone's attention. I looked back and saw the group fanatically point to one of their teammates: a woman who appeared to be in her twenties and seemed embarrassed and nervous at the spectacle being made about her. She was hesitant to come up, but her team was so adamant they all decided to walk up to the stage so she would have to follow them. Once on stage, the Master Coach asked her about herself. While still visibly nervous and anxious, she shared that she was scared to speak in group settings. After some coaching, she soon accepted that beneath her fear of speaking was a fear of not wanting to be seen, which you could see in her disposition since she was cowering in one place, almost trying to be invisible.

At this point, the Master Coach directed her to change her physiology and do the exact opposite - to stand tall, face the thousand-plus audience with arms open wide like a starfish, and allow herself to be vulnerable and fully seen. Her fear and hesitation were real; she looked like she wanted to run off stage. But with her team behind her cheering her on, she got out of the spectacle of that moment and locked eyes with them. You could see her return to the present moment and find courage in their belief in her. Then something truly magical happened. It was like the entire audience understood that split-second, non-verbal dialogue that had just occurred between her and her team. And within moments, we all joined in, encouraging her with screams, shouts, chants, and cheers. Her face became filled with gratitude and wonder at the strangers showing her love. She even broke out with a huge smile and began crying. You could see her fear disappear as she received the energy we gave her. She then stood tall and opened up her arms so she could be fully seen, and we roared again to celebrate her victory over herself.

That interaction grounded me in the power of love across boundaries. It was amazing to witness complete strangers stand in the gap for another stranger simply because we wanted her to achieve the vision of greatness she had for herself.

If you haven't ever attended a Tony Robbins event, I strongly recommend it. The community and culture they create are like no other. It is hundreds or thousands of complete strangers with a shared desire to rise up from their situations and be their best; everyone smiling at each other, greeting each other with hugs, treating each other like old friends, without judgment, and with full acceptance. It literally feels like heaven on earth.

Relationship with God

I believe a relationship with God not only enables all relationships in our lives to be optimized but also enables us to reach our greatest expression, which is self-actualization and purpose. This is because God is Love and Spirit, and that is also who we are. Therefore, drawing close to God essentially draws us closer to ourselves. It is the beginning of an awakening, a self-discovery.

This world trains us to give others or objects the power to make us happy. However, when we give this power away, we are eventually disappointed because certain circumstances in life and people are flawed. I've found the best place to put my contentment is in someone or something perfect and everlasting so that I can never be disappointed and can be full of love for myself and others at all times, especially when situations trigger the Human side of me. That perfect being for me is God. As much as we want our spouses, partners, children, and loved ones to fill us or complete us, the reality is they are human and, at some point, will disappoint us or not be able to meet that expectation. I have experienced that when I have a strong connection with God and myself as Spirit, I am able to be full of joy, regardless of people or circumstances. And in my humble opinion, joy is always greater than happiness.

I reconnected with God in my adult life because I found myself in a low period, and reaching out to Him was a matter of necessity and survival for me. As Humans, we easily tend to spend our entire lives trying to avoid pain and struggle when it is those exact moments that allow us that chance to lean on God and witness His power and love. Just like going through tough times with family or friends brings you closer together, that same closeness can be found with God. Our faith can't grow if we don't exercise and stretch our faith through overcoming challenges. Compare this to working out. Our muscles won't improve without weight training. If we don't work out our faith and challenge and push it to new levels, it not only won't grow, we will experience atrophy.

This is how I've reprogrammed myself. I now get excited about challenges because I see them as a sign of God's exponential love for me. When He sees me reach a comfort zone and wants to show me yet another depth and the breadth of His power and love, He allows a challenge to come to me. Growing through this situation or event will provide insights and skills I can use to love others in an even greater way.

> *"'For I know the plans I have for you,' says the Lord, 'plans to prosper you and not to harm you. Plans to give you hope and a future.'"*
>
> *-Jeremiah 29:11 (NIV)*

When it comes to loving others, especially when I have every reason to not be loving, Jesus gives me an example to follow. I think of how Jesus forgave those who crucified him IN THE MOMENT. It sounds like words on a page to us who have never witnessed first-hand a torturing or an execution. Think of the greatest pain someone has caused you. Now consider that IN THAT MOMENT of that pain, you could fully and whole-heartedly have love and empathy. You could forgive that person because you recognize the flawed state of humans. They hurt you because they are hurt and don't know how to love because they haven't experienced love. The lack of love is a real thing. Lust is when we fail to love and whenever our focus is placed on what we're not getting, whether or not we are the one at fault.

So, here is an example of how I apply this. Let's say someone does or says something to me that is rude or offensive. Naturally, I'd want to counter back and say or do something equally as rude or offensive, if not more, to protect myself and check that person. It's in this moment of negative emotion that I train myself to pause and become present and get out of my head, which is full of upset and frustration. I choose to activate my Spirit identity. I then recall Jesus, justified in feeling anger and rage towards His killers while still having and holding love for them. He realizes they are flawed and are not even conscious of the driving forces behind the subsequent impact of their actions.

I remember that if Jesus can choose love at that moment, surely I can choose love in mine. And even though I don't feel love in my heart, I choose it and act accordingly. That may mean calmly and lovingly voicing what I think or feel. It may mean not saying anything and walking away. It may mean focusing on the other person's pain and suffering and seeing how I can help them. The humbling moment is always after I take loving action. I realize how the veil of negative emotion that was once over me lifts and disappears so I can see things clearly for what they are instead of the "lustful" story I created in my head. In this way, I choose love, not lust, and embrace my Spirit state while letting go of my Human one.

I understand many people reading my book do not believe in a specific God or any kind of God at all. I absolutely respect their perspective.

AND I also adamantly know, without a shadow of a doubt, because I'm a testament to it, that your life experience will elevate you to levels you never imagined when you get to intimately and actively know God or whatever you identify as a higher power or source in your life. But let's say this is all bologna, and there isn't such an entity as God. What would it mean for you and your life experience to access levels of greatness, power, freedom, peace, and joy that you can only dream of? Isn't just that possibility worth exploring a relationship with God? The best-case scenario is that you will experience the love, joy, freedom, and abundance He promises and gives to us. If your answer is still "No, thank you," my follow-up question to consider is, "What makes you afraid to try if there is nothing to lose and everything to gain?"

I encourage you to practice faith and expectancy because when you cannot activate faith, you cannot come to know yourself as Spirit. And it is in this Unbecoming of Spirit that you will also come to know God because the Spirit within us is connected to the Spirit outside of us.

Relationship with Children

"Heal before you have children so your children don't have to heal from having you as a parent'"

-Unknown

When you read that quote from me, what did you hear? Did you hear that our children are gifts to this world if they grow up to be doctors or lawyers or some other title that is seen as prestigious? Or make sure we raise decent human beings? Or help kids achieve every dream we were never able to?

I believe our children are our greatest gifts to the world because of the power and wisdom they possess. And it is our job as adults to stop thinking and acting like we are wiser than them. We need to teach them our ways because many of our ways are subconsciously programmed into us at a young age and reinforce our identity as Humans instead of as Spirits. Our jobs as caregivers are to be aware of our own Human condition and let children be their true Spirit selves. We should not impose our expectations of what we think they should be but teach them from a place of divine love, not learned trauma.

Allow me to give one example: extracurricular activities for kids. I know some parents are self-aware and allow their kids to voice their interests and thoughts and choose the extracurricular activities they like. But that is not the case for everyone. Do we put our children into multiple activities because of our love for them or because of a fear or limiting belief instilled in us at a young age? Or because of a need we have that we were not able to fulfill in our own childhood? Our children are similar to us, but they are not us. Our children come through us, but we do not own them. Parenting is hard work, and I see so many parents suffer more than necessary through parenthood because of the Lust (again, platonic in nature) and Ego they allow in the parent-child relationship. I'm guilty of it, too. It's part of our Human nature. The key is to be mindful of this nature, so we can pivot our words and actions at the moment and choose what will nurture our children's gifts and passions over our expectations of what we want them to do.

In Matthew 18 (NIV), the answer to "The Greatest in the Kingdom of Heaven" speaks of the Spirit state where children are the masters: "At that time the disciples came to Jesus and asked, 'Who, then, is the greatest in the kingdom of heaven?' He called a little child to him, and placed the child among them. And he said: 'Truly I tell you, **unless you change and become like little children**, you will never enter the kingdom of heaven. Therefore, whoever takes the lowly position of this child is the greatest in the kingdom of heaven. And whoever welcomes one such child in my name welcomes me.'"

Additionally, 1 Corinthians 13: 9-12 (NIV) says, "For we know in part and we prophesy in part, but when completeness comes, what is in part disappears. When I was a child, I talked like a child, I thought like a child, I reasoned like a child. When I became a man, I put the ways of childhood behind me. For now we see only a reflection as in a mirror; then we shall see face to face." We must intentionally respect, love, and nurture our children's unique identities and journeys. In fact, we can find power in respecting their wisdom and even allow them to awaken our Spirit and help us to Unbecome and go back to our child-like selves in the process of raising them.

One last teaching I'll share is about our energy as parents and how our children absorb and emit that same energy back out, along with the corresponding emotion. A few commonplace examples of where I see this show up is during transition periods, like learning to eat, sleep training, potty training, and starting school. There is a strong correlation or likeness between a parent's energy and their children's. If you see your child anxious about or resistant to starting school or sleep training, there is a high probability they are reflecting the energy you are giving off back to you. So if you're a parent, mindfully model the energy and emotion you want your child to operate with.

"Our children are our greatest gifts to this world."

-Rowen Labuguen Turner

Marriage

I titled this section Marriage since it is the most challenging of all romantic relationships because, ideally and theoretically, it is a commitment forever. However, the content within this section also applies to serious, romantic relationships, as I've come to realize many married couples don't hold love for one another, while many unmarried couples do.

Marriages are wonderful growth opportunities because, in a marriage, two people are essentially saying to the world that no matter what, I will choose to stick it out with you, another flawed human being. But first, allow me to insert a caveat here. I understand there are instances where you should not stick it out because of concerns for safety or well-being. Please know I am not talking about those relationships.

But looking back, what I know now was at the core of my suffering in a previous relationship that tricked me into staying for way too long was my own deluded belief of what a relationship should be. I was fooled into believing an earthly world's definition of a romantic relationship, depicted by the fairytales and soap operas we see at a young age. The bold and ubiquitous lie that the person I choose to build a life with should be my everything. They should have the same interests, friends, dreams, and belief system, show love the same way I do, and on and on and on. Whether we like it or not, because the fairytale or soap opera is so prevalent, it becomes the perceived norm we compare our circumstances to. And that expectation and pressure put upon our partner, the expectation of what that relationship should look like, creates our suffering. I'm not saying we can't have a dream for what we want our person or relationship to be like. We can, just not at the cost of being disillusioned and now looking at our person and relationship from a Lust perspective of "What am I getting?" versus a Love perspective of "What am I giving?" and "Who am I becoming?" during the relationship.

Love is when two different people, because we are all magnificently unique, can live life together, fully embracing and loving their similarities and differences daily. Because that is what Love is.

First, let's talk about what we look for when searching for love. I think it's odd how we hope to find the perfect love the first time. Those kinds of love stories exist, but most happen after a few or more practice rounds. To stay in Spirit in a romantic relationship, enjoying the adventure is critical, instead of trying to get to the "stable" and "certain" end too fast. Nothing in this world is stable or certain. Many times, romantic relationships are about learning what love is. It is about staying in exploration mode and having fun discovering another person and yourself while watching the story unfold.

Second, let's talk about another very common question: how do you know he or she is "the one?" I can tell you it's not what you see in movies or fairy tales, where they present the "ideal" relationships with emotional highs and lows, a lot of spectacle, excitement, and a "wow" factor. Here is the hard truth. That kind of scenario depicts Lust, not Love. Referring back to the duality grid, Love is all of the things mentioned in the left-hand column. It is secure, peaceful, gratifying, forgiving, and selfless.

I'll share my personal experience with my husband. I knew he was the one when I realized I felt secure and joyful with him. Because of my past, I brought in a lot of unnecessary turbulence in our beginning years. Still, through it all, I could see myself building a solid future together with him. I saw him as not only my best friend but also a partner.

Because of that relationship, the last thing I want to share is the biggest thing I learned about love with my husband. To give some background, we met through my BFFFL (Best Friend Forever For Life). We started as friends, and I fell in love with his loyalty, honesty, confidence, and consistency. We dated long-distance for four years. He was in Las Vegas and then Boston while I was in Hawaii. I finally joined him in Massachusetts after I finished graduate school at the University of Hawaii at Manoa Shidler College of Business and discovered that being around each other more often was different for us. Up until that point, whenever we were together, roughly one week every three months, we had experienced the best of each other because we were both in "vacation mode" during our trips. Being consistently around each other was a new dynamic for us. We got to experience what each other was like at our worst. As most couples fall into this trap, there was a fair amount of blaming each other for the tension in our relationship. In reading Gary Chapman's *The 5 Love Languages: The Secret to Love that Lasts*, we learned that our love languages are different - my primary love language is "Words of Affirmation," while his is "Acts of Service." So we were showing love to each other but not receiving or perceiving the efforts.

As our love story moved forward, we failed to uncover the root issues, and fighting over the symptoms made things worse. So much so that we contemplated and threatened to call it quits. Feeling in my Spirit that we had to try everything possible to make it work between us, I asked him to join me for couple's counseling. He wasn't open to it at first because going to counseling was unfamiliar for both of us. But ultimately, our relationship had gotten so rocky he finally agreed to go.

I was curious about how this would go. And sadly, I was fully prepared for the realization that we might have to end things. Once our counselor got to know us, he asked us what we thought the issue was. We both stated that we had communication issues. But, he respectfully challenged back, asserting we were both great at communicating, evidenced by the fact that we both were successful professionals who effectively communicated daily at work. He leaned further and shared how he sees countless couples with problems. However, he thought we didn't have problems; we were creating them. He referenced the idea that successful relationships don't just happen because of chemistry; it takes good old-fashioned hard work and compromise. He further challenged us by saying, "If you want to be together, then decide to be together and be willing to do some give and take. Find ways to make it work. Stop fighting each other and start working together to find the solution."

I would say it was a profound session because a couple hours after we got home, my husband proposed, and I said, "Yes." And the rest has been joyful work. (My husband recalls this series of events differently, but that's a story for another time.) Over the next several months leading up to our wedding, I intentionally prepared my heart and mind for marriage. I knew marriage was just the beginning of the journey, and there would naturally be challenges. So I wanted to practice and train. I read the book *Sacred Marriage: What if God Designed Marriage to Make Us More Holy Than to Make Us More Happy?* during this time, and its teachings transformed my view on how I approached my relationship. The question on the book's cover asks, "What if God designed marriage to make us holy more than to make us happy?" I learned how to see each interaction with Marcus as an opportunity to grow in love. But I also used it as an indicator of my relationship with God, sometimes even more so than with my marital relationship. This book helped me unlearn what I thought love was and re-learn what love truly is, as described in 1 Corinthians above.

I really gave my all to this relationship transformation. I considered everything I could do to make it better, as well as everything I was doing that hurt it. My nagging and criticizing of how my husband did things, or pointing out things that I thought he should be doing, are examples of how I hurt the relationship.

IBAO

In the "Goal Digging" chapter, I discussed the limiting beliefs that come into play when achieving a goal. To counter this, I wanted to create a process to help me move beyond these limits. And with that in mind, I came up with IBAO to help me Unbecome with a specific goal.

IBAO stands for:

Identity + **B**eliefs → Determines **A**ctions → Delivers **O**utcomes

Let me share how I applied my IBAO principle to this scenario. The most effective way to do this exercise is backward because we are only sometimes aware and clear of the Identity and Beliefs we operate from. So we start with the Outcome, dig into the Actions that yield it, then the Beliefs and Identity at the core of it all. Let's take a look at how this develops in the following chart.

	Desired State	**Current State**
Outcome	To have a loving and joyful relationship with my then-boyfriend (now husband). A future where, as my husband and when asked about me, I'd see him lighting up with joy and excitement, not annoyance or frustration. Then I imagined him sharing how much he appreciates things I do and enjoys spending time with me. I envisioned being a source of love, peace, and joy for him.	Regular tension in our relationship. He feels he must be a certain way with me or meet my expectations. I feel like I have to watch and care for him like a kid.
Action	Focus on his many strengths, be grateful for them, and enjoy his company fully.	At the time, I was nagging. I mainly focused on his opportunities and offered constructive feedback or made complaints.
Belief	When you love someone, you don't try to control them.	When you love someone, you give them feedback so they can be better.
Identity	Girlfriend, Future Wife, Partner	Second Mom

In the "Goal Digging" chapter, I mentioned the best practice of finding a role model that has already achieved your desired outcome is to identify their identity, beliefs, and actions. My role model for this was Jesus and how He could act lovingly towards his murderers, even while he was dying. Even though this may seem extreme, I knew that if Jesus could love his enemies, surely I could love my husband through our disagreements.

Doing this exercise turned on many lightbulbs for me, even from prior relationships. I thought like most girlfriends or wives do of their boyfriends or husbands. There were times when I believed my husband was acting like a child I had to correct, not because of his behaviors but because of the identity I embraced as needing to be his Mom versus his Wife. I'm not sure to this day why I had the two confused, but I feel like many women have this same disconnect. There is something innate in women that triggers us to think and act like a Mom in some instances and not like a partner, cheerleader, and lover. And when our partner responds by treating us like a parent, we wonder why.

Disagreements

I wanted to recall a fact that helps me when I find myself worked up emotionally over a disagreement with anyone. In Pragya Agarwal's study mentioned in the "Religion and Self-Transformation" chapter, at least 11 million plus bits of information hit our senses every second. In that time, we can only process about 50 of them a second. That means in any given situation, we, at most, see less than 1% of the situation, if that. Yet, we take our 50 bits of perspective to heart and hold others to it as if it was the entire 11 million bits pictured. Data shows that when someone else says something you disagree with, it is not necessarily that they are wrong. There is a very high likelihood that what the other person is saying IS true. But it just happens to be something you can't perceive because it is in the other 10,999,950 bits of information you couldn't process.

The Skill of Surrender

Surrender means "to accept or yield to a superior force or to the authority or will of another person" (Merriam-Webster, n.d.). The context of this word can be negative for some, as it has almost evolved to include a storyline that the one who is surrendering is weak or less than the one being surrendered to. When in fact, all it is saying is that one is accepting or giving way to someone or something greater than them. What is considered superior or authority can be left open to interpretation. I think this is where issues can arise, and there may be resistance, reservation, or even repulsion to surrendering.

For me, surrendering in the context of a healthy relationship is in the mental and emotional versus the physical sense. The time it takes to surrender to the Godly, loving action and not the human, self-preserving one is what causes a delay in a resolution, breakthrough, or promise. I believe this is the very same dynamic that caused the Israelites to be delayed by forty years of wandering the desert on their way to the Promised Land. Theologians teach how their journey could have been completed in forty days. Yet, they gave in to their human condition and remained lost for over a generation.

Surrendering to God and surrendering to love can be difficult and sometimes also feel impossible because our human brains are programmed to be ego-centric for survival. Generally, what is at the top of our minds in a moment of conflict is that we are right and the other party is wrong. We don't see another way because we simply are so engulfed in our own perspective that we are incapable of seeing anyone else's.

The unlocking of surrender is knowing that the next step, the right step, is always the loving action (reference the Duality grid as needed). Our brains tempt our Human self and trick us into seeing and believing the self-serving, easier alternatives as viable because it is fulfilling its role as self-protector. Training ourselves to Unbecome and choose love, in spite of any reason or obstacle, takes practice, as well as a genuine desire to be and grow in love through God.

Once you surrender, ease happens almost immediately. It is the energy and possibility that surrender opens the way for. It's a shift in energy. In overcoming our flesh, we activate the spiritual realm and take abundant action.

Relationships

All relationships have a course to run. Some are for a lifetime, many a season, and others for a moment. There are times throughout the course of a relationship when tension comes up. Some difficult times may result in considering ending the relationship. Here are questions that may help you decide if a relationship is truly no longer serving you and allowing you to be your highest self. Or if your Human self is being triggered because you aren't getting something you want.

- Why did I get into this relationship? Does that person still have that quality or trait that attracted me in the first place?
    - If so, when did my expectation of that person change?
    - If not, how have I given the feedback with love to that person?
- Does this desired or undesired behavior from this person upset you when someone else does (or doesn't do) it?
    - If not, why do you let it bother you or find that it is this person's deficit?
    - Why must this person, versus all people, uphold this expectation for you??
- Is this want or need that you are not getting from this person something you should be giving yourself?

This world has trained us to believe that others are in charge of our happiness. However, I've found that is not true. Happiness is fleeting because it is influenced by the external environment. Joy is eternal because it is internal, originating from knowing who you are. You have complete control over it.

Women as the Spiritual Leader of the Household

I will start this section by first acknowledging that this could become a highly controversial topic. As a highly ambitious, independent woman myself, I have toiled many years of understanding the power women have. I have an ask for you as we go through this section. I pray you read it with a blank slate. Try to remain in Spirit and keep the meanings and experiences you've had about the word and identity of "woman" at bay as you process the personal reflections I share. In fact, you might even want to remove the visual or physical ties to the word by using the Taoist term Yin, or feminine energy. Please note that this section is not a dissertation or explanation of what is or is not woman or female. That is not my area of personal understanding or experience. My belief is that as physical human beings, there is a tangible difference we can see and acknowledge in the physical body's anatomy. Additionally, as divine, spiritual beings, there is no tangible difference between men and women; we are the same and hold the same energetic power and ability. It is our human form that creates an earthly limitation to our capabilities.

I have come to understand that women, as sources of feminine, yin energy in this world, are incredibly powerful, spiritual beings. I'll go so far as to say that we are the energy and spiritual leaders and protectors of our home and this universe. It is part of our masterful design and role in this world, regardless of whether we want that responsibility. Therefore our actions, whether intentional about them or not, bear fruit that has ripple effects on events and those around us. I believe this divine power that women have is strongly tied to the ability to create and bring forth life.

Now for the part of my experience that may trigger my fellow independent women. There is a perspective in the world that women should submit or be obedient to their husbands. That triggers so much emotion, if not anger, in many or most women. I read once from a female Italian author how when we hear "under or beneath," we visualize that as a rug to be walked all over. Instead, could we see our role of being "under or beneath" as pillars: strong in love, able to endure and persevere and never give up, which like God, is the definition of love?

Subservience or obedience to God, not to another human being, means surrendering to God's way. For example, my most significant experience with practicing surrender was with my husband. I shared above how we had gone through some hard times and blamed it on our ineffective communication. To get myself out of this blaming cycle and see if there was anything else I could be doing to change our situation, I asked myself the hard question: "Do I want the dream" or "Do I care more that it happens my way?" So I gave God's way a try, and I was absolutely floored with awe and humility when I saw it work. I realized what I had done in choosing God's way was to kill my human ego, my human desire to be right and control the situation. I realized it had nothing to do with my husband and everything to do with my journey to draw closer to God by becoming more loving and forgiving. I needed to become more like God and surrender to His way.

Understanding and then mastering surrender is likely the most challenging thing I practice. And when it gets hard, especially when it feels near impossible, I call on those I know and those through history who have been able to overcome the impossible. For me, I often call on Jesus Christ. He reminds me I can do all things through Him who strengthens me. He endured things I don't think I could, and He was human like us. Like us, He was also divine. It reminds me that we can activate our Spirit and do anything.

And it's not to say women only have to surrender. Women are the source of a love energy that is at the core of surrender, so we are naturally more equipped to do so. It is through our loving surrender that we remind both women and men that we are Spirit. We hold the power that loving surrender has to our experience in this life and the energy in our world.

Before we close out this chapter, let's do a quick exercise. In the numbered spaces, take a few moments to name all the people and/or things you love.

1. _____

2. _____

3. _____

4. _____

5. _____

6. _____

7. _____

8. _____

9. _____

10. _____

Were you able to fill up all twenty slots? How long did it take for you to name *yourself*? If you didn't have yourself down, is it because loving "Me" is something you feel uncomfortable with? Why?

When I first did this exercise, "Me" was not even something on my radar that I would think to write. I considered that even if you were full of self-love, there's a good chance you wouldn't put yourself down. But then I challenged myself to consider that if loving myself was top of mind for me, I would have to put it down, just like I did God, my husband, my boys, my family, etc. Rest assured that just because you don't put yourself down doesn't mean you don't love yourself at all; it simply means there is a gap in the extent you love yourself and the possible optimal level. In the next section, we'll explore more about this idea of self-love.

Chapter 14

Esteem, Career, and Achievement

Esteem

Esteem is defined as respect and admiration for a person (Oxford Languages, n.d.). So self-esteem would be having respect and admiration for yourself. I believe at the core of self-esteem is self-love.

We learn how to love and value others by watching how our parents and caregivers show love to themselves and others. The issue is that our parents and caregivers, and their parents and caregivers and so on, are all flawed human beings. Therefore, we all have a gap in knowing what real, divine, unconditional love looks and feels like, and this gap shows up in our ability to love ourselves fully. Now, when I say love "yourself," I am speaking about you as Spirit - your true, authentic, child-like self, rather than the limited Human you physically see in the mirror. Love yourself daily because it is unreasonable to expect someone else who is also flawed and has to take care of themselves first to love you back.

I struggled with this idea of self-love because selflessness has long been a key trait for me. My natural tendency to care for others was so strong that I couldn't see the gap it created in caring for myself first, thereby limiting the level of love I could give others. In fact, I couldn't comprehend how to truly balance the two. Thinking of caring for myself felt selfish. The disconnect in my brain was thinking that if I chose myself in any given situation, that would somehow undo all the selflessness I had done prior to that and make me the MOST selfish person in the world. Totally unrealistic, right? But that was literally the thought in my head. The sad truth is we have many of those incorrect deductions that we follow that limit our ability to self-actualize and express ourselves while living at the highest level possible. For example, if there was a discussion about what I wanted to eat for dinner, I would almost always defer to what my friends, family, or co-workers wanted because of my habit of caring for others. However, in not sharing my opinion, I was inadvertently telling myself I mattered less. Loving yourself means expressing your needs and desires. So the way I approach this scenario now is to share my perspective and, if I really do want something, to express it. It does not mean I will get what I want at that moment, but I am loving myself enough to acknowledge myself, which helps me feel as valuable as those I care for.

Remember that love is action, not feeling. Let's repeat that because I know we hear this many times but don't always truly understand and live in this truth. I see many people and relationships suffer because we don't FEEL love and waste time and energy on ways to get that FEELING. We wallow in the lack of FEELING loved. But Love is also ACTION. Love is ACTION. Love is ACTION! Wallowing and complaining prevent us from taking ACTION, and we can get stuck in a state of lacking love as a fleeting byproduct. When you find you don't have love to the degree you desire, then decide to ACT with Love and be Love. And then you will find you can create it.

It is critical we learn to love ourselves. Only through full self-love can we reach our greatest expression and be our true selves, our inner child, and our Spirit.

"I don't really care if everybody likes me, I just want to love myself."

-Grace Davis (Tracee Ellis Ross), The High Note

After reading this quote, most people I know get energized by the reminder to love themselves. The energy you hold when you acknowledge this statement makes a difference. I've heard this sentiment in two different ways. One is with anger, resentment, defensiveness, and division in our hearts: this is us saying it through our Human self. Another way is to say it with peace, joy, abundance, love, and empathy for those who we feel don't like us: this is saying it through our Spirit.

When I did the "name all the people and/or things you love" exercise for the first time, I didn't write myself down. Raise your hand or smile if you're like me. If you did write yourself down, I admire and respect you for prioritizing yourself. Looking back, I realized I didn't put my name down, not because I didn't love myself at all, but because I had room to love myself more. I also became very curious about how my world would change if I could program myself to make myself a priority. How much more would my quality of life and my relationships with others be enhanced?

Here is a powerful truth. When we Unbecome, we see that our natural, child-like state as Spirit provides unconditional love for ourselves. Babies aren't born wondering why their skin is darker or lighter or why they are missing a limb. They don't compare themselves to other babies because they are in a state of Love and acceptance for what is. When a child begins to compare themselves, that is a notable time in their development. As a parent, it makes me reflect on what I might do or say about myself that may teach my children to make the same comparisons.

As I dug into this for myself, I realized my opportunity for self-love, or lack thereof, started at a young age from various seemingly meaningless instances. One such instance is because of the darker color of my skin. In Filipino culture, as well as the broader Asian culture, we have somehow adopted the belief that lighter skin is prettier. In fact, you'll see many Asians cover up in the sun to prevent themselves from tanning. Some Filipinos take it even further by using a popular product called Eskinol that helps lighten their skin. At the moment, I didn't realize the impact it had on me. Still, in reflection, I realize it added to my belief that because I had darker skin, I was not beautiful.

Another example is how embarrassed I felt when someone couldn't say or spell my name correctly. I tended to focus on making it easier for the person by letting them pronounce it wrong instead of teaching them how to pronounce it correctly. By doing this, I didn't help others like me with similar names feel accepted for who they were. Instead, I enabled the feeling that they needed to have an American name, too. Thinking about this, the biggest insight was how much of a surprise this gap was for me. At the time, I didn't necessarily believe that these were indicators that self-love was an issue for me. I needed to learn that just because I didn't have a major life event that impacted me negatively didn't mean that I didn't have a blaring gap of self-love in my life due to what is now identifiable as obviously destructive behavior. Having experienced these two examples of not loving myself for myself, I knew I was more motivated than ever to discover the new heights of self-love that actually existed. But I hadn't had the wisdom or growth to experience that yet.

This break in self-love and self-esteem showed up in my romantic relationships. At a high level, I found myself in relationships where I wasn't treated the best. And now, I see that I attracted partners that matched the same level of self-love I demonstrated for myself. It wasn't until I fully understood and accepted this flawed perspective within my own human nature that I could love myself and extend love, empathy, and forgiveness to others.

I also connect esteem to a person's ability to dream. There are many people in the world who don't have the opportunity to realize their dreams because their energy has to be focused on meeting basic human needs, like putting food on the table and staying physically safe. So I always remember that while I have plans of abundance for my future, I am also incredibly grateful for all that I currently have.

I remember an experience I had one day during a hostess shift at Morton's Steakhouse. I noticed every walk of life entering the restaurant to look at the menu or join us for a meal. When seating them, some explained that eating at such a prestigious steakhouse wasn't something they had ever imagined for themselves. Even though this is a simple example, it proves that big dreams can come in different sizes, and even a "smaller" dream can be realized by anyone. So, I strive to inspire and encourage others to dream like a child again. Then once you give yourself that permission, have the faith to dream BIG. Love yourself. Be your own cheerleader despite the naysayers or past programming you may have.

Another powerful learning I had regarding my own struggles with self-esteem occurred when I became aware that I avoided attention, especially on my birthday or any other event where I was the center of it. I shied away from birthday greetings, especially ones that were a bit "extra." Even being sung to at restaurants put me ill at ease. Having the spotlight placed upon me has always made me uneasy, and I can now see that at the core of this discomfort with attention was a gap in self-love. I could never fully receive these well wishes and celebrations because some part of me didn't believe I was worthy of them. This may be surprising to hear for people who know me well because, on the surface or even in my subconsciousness, it seemed like I did have a healthy sense of esteem and self-love. However, regardless of this uneasiness, I knew I could change my thinking and my life by taking a different ACTION.

For my birthday this year, I mustered up the courage to do a birthday post on all my social media accounts, which was the exact opposite of what I wanted to do. Man, was I sweating and hesitating all the way through. Every time I found myself wussing out, I reminded myself that person was the old Rowen, who felt incapable of loving herself to the fullest. And because I wanted to know what would happen if I unlocked the ability within me to love myself fully, I did it, even though I was afraid. I know, it sounds so silly now. But, by posting it, I opened a new world of possibility for myself. Posting about my birthday was a symbolic action that proved the old, insecure me was in the past and the new, loved, and confident me could and would exist whenever I chose.

To build on this "aha moment," I had an insightful breakthrough at a seminar I attended the weekend after my birthday. It was Landmark Forum's Advanced Course, whose goal for their attendees was to "Create a future of your own design, not limited by the past. Move the notion of possibility from an abstract idea to a day-to-day living reality."

Through the coaching, I saw that ever since I was about seven years old, I lived by a rule that "in order to receive love, I needed to be perfect and be seen as perfect." As a result, I experienced a lot of pain in my life because I relied on others to love me instead of learning how to love myself fully and completely. I suffered even more because I set an unfair, unrealistic, and unhealthy burden on myself to be perfect. Now being aware of it, I can see how it added so much stress to my life and kept me from enjoying each moment.

One last personal example regarding my lack of self-esteem was staying in a job where I felt depleted almost every day, even though I seemed OK from the outside. I was burned out, constantly working sixty to seventy hours a week. The sad part was that I didn't even realize how stressed and pressured I was because I had gotten so used to it. I tolerated a bad working environment that drained me mentally and spiritually but stuck with it for many reasons. One of those reasons was that I loved my business partner, team, and co-workers dearly. I didn't want to let them down by leaving during a really challenging period. Plus, I was torn by the notion that leaving my job would mean that I wasn't loyal. It meant that I was a quitter, not good enough or strong enough to hack it like everyone else.

If I'm really being honest with myself, I stayed longer than I should have because I let myself be tempted by my dreams of moving up the corporate ladder and bringing my ideas to life within the company. I was tempted by the perceived clout and status in the business world that comes from being with a big brand and by the lure of getting to the next level and gaining the financial benefits that would come with it.

I actively wrestled with this decision for a couple of years. I felt stuck for a while, trying everything and anything within my power to bring joy and fun back to my work. I became more vocal about my work experience. I shared ideas about how we needed to change to improve the day-to-day culture and work experience for employees. I took on projects, new roles, and temporary assignments to increase the power of my opinion. But how I felt, unfortunately, only got worse. I was pushing for culture transformation in an organization that just wasn't in the position to truly transform for various reasons. I became increasingly frustrated by the lack of courage to take action on the initiatives that would truly make a difference for employees rather than shareholders.

Then the truth hit me so clearly one day: only I had the power to free myself from this environment all along. But instead of loving myself and choosing my health, and mental and physical well-being, I chose the comfort of my current situation and the duty I had to others. When I finally made the decision to end my almost fourteen-year run with my company, I experienced a FREEDOM, JOY, and POWER I hadn't felt in years. I didn't realize how constrained I was until I realized how free and alive I had felt after leaving. It was an incredible lesson about loving myself more than money and making myself a priority.

Finding and Seeing Your Value

Seeing the value we hold has a strong correlation with our ability to love ourselves fully. A critical factor in the value we see in ourselves is our identity. If I asked you, "Who are you?", what would you answer? I want you to take a moment and ask yourself now.

Reflection Question: Who are you? Use "I AM…" to start each sentence.

Reflection Question: What did you think and feel as you created and wrote "I AM" statements? What did you learn about yourself and your sense of identity?

When I first did this exercise, I listed a few things. My answers were about the roles I play in life, the job I have, and the traits I use on a daily basis. It was an odd exercise for me because I hadn't intentionally or outwardly thought about my identity before. My answers didn't necessarily inspire or energize me; they were simply a matter of fact. Having done work around self-esteem and love over the last couple of years, I have since seen my answers evolve. I feel more clarity and conviction when I respond. I get energized by reminding myself of my identity. I've learned that our identity can be whatever we want it to be at any given moment and that whatever we choose is our way of being. As we elevate to purpose, you'll find that your identity transcends your physical nature. My answers evolved from "I AM" a wife, mom, business leader, and HR professional to "I AM" God's daughter and one of his greatest warriors of all time who is filled with Love, Integrity, Freedom, Divinity, and Possibility.

Value from What Others Think

I am fascinated by how hardwired we are to place value in what others think of us. First, we value what our parents think of us. Eventually, we also value what our friends, teachers, partners, bosses, and whoever else has importance in our life think about us. While this serves a primitive purpose in our survival, it can also cause suffering if we lose awareness of the power we give others.

One of the biggest ways I've seen this show up in my life is through my grades in school and my performance ratings at work. My historical programming placed an unhealthy, excessive value on those ratings. I grew up thinking that an "A" grade wasn't good enough. It had to be an A+ to count. But even if that "A+" was 98%, I would spend unnecessary energy obsessing over what I could have done differently to get 100%. I remember when I was a freshman in my high school's English Honors class, and we had to write a one-page essay about ourselves. I obsessed so much about needing it to be a perfect A+, a 100%, that I worked myself up into an anxiety attack. Thank goodness I got an A+ grade and was so relieved that I shared my experience with my teacher. She gave me a pep talk about how learning something was always the main objective in any assignment and to remove the pressure from myself about getting a particular grade. I believe her pep talk made a difference for me because I saw her as highly intelligent with incredibly high standards, and I was moved by her warmth when speaking with me. I could feel that she saw me as a bright student regardless of my grades, and her grace and love planted a new kind of seed for me. One that would help me slowly but surely reprogram how I valued myself twenty years later.

Even with this planted seed, the deeply ingrained connection between my self-worth and performance rating carried over when I entered the workforce. I didn't realize how much value I placed in the rating my leader gave me until I didn't get an "exceeds expectations" on my evaluation. I thought I had overcome this human tendency for approval during my twenties. But recently, I was painfully reminded how deeply rooted this need in me was. I had shared before how I suffered from "trying-to-be-perfect" syndrome. So naturally, how I performed at work mattered a lot to me. Luckily, I had a leader who cared so much about me that she explained why I couldn't get an "exceeds expectations" or "outstanding performance" every year. Yet, while I heard her, I still believed differently. It wasn't the end of the world. Unfortunately, by not getting the performance rating I felt I deserved, it did feel that way. But her wisdom sat in my heart, and I'm so grateful for it because it cushioned the experience. And as an HR professional, I tell my leaders, who are also overachievers, that "meets expectations" can be a great thing and to remember that you are NOT your performance. This doesn't mean that it's OK to not perform. It means we shouldn't tie our identity to our performance because we can consciously make the choice to take action towards or away from our goals.

Career and Achievement

> *"Best career advice that I can give: Don't ever attach yourself to a person, a place, a company, an organization or a project. Attach yourself to a mission, a calling, a purpose ONLY. That's how you keep your power & your peace."*
>
> -Erica Williams Simon

We are so used to being pressured that we cannot even fathom or comprehend what freedom actually feels like. We get so used to operating with restraints that we become immune and forget that we even have them holding us back or weighing us down.

If you define yourself as "driven," you likely push yourself to always do the most. There is nothing inherently wrong with pushing yourself to do more. But when the cost to achieve more is your health and well-being, your joy on a regular basis, your relationships, and your ability to truly enjoy the present moment for all that it is, you need to make a change. And if you're doing all of this in a career you don't love, then you must find the courage to let go of what no longer serves you.

Now keep in mind that a possible risk with leaning into doing just enough instead of doing the most is that we could become lazy or lose productivity or progress. I believe we can mitigate, if not eliminate, this risk by bravely choosing work that aligns with our gifts, talents, passion, and purpose. To work on something that means so much to you because you love the work itself, and not just the money, status, or certainty it may give you, has incomprehensible value. You could wake up every morning with eagerness and excitement to take on the day. If you don't wake up with that level of enthusiasm and love for the life you have now, then I would assert you are still, to some extent, playing in just the esteem, career, and achievement level. Nothing is wrong with that. But, I want to simply draw awareness and point out that lack of enthusiasm indicates you are not yet at purpose. So keep leaning in, and you will soon discover how to unlock your transition into purpose while using your gifts to discover your value in this world.

Hearing Your Inner Voice

An essential tool to guide you towards healthy self-esteem and purposeful, fulfilling work and goals is the ability to hear your inner voice. You can call this intuition, the God in you, the Holy Spirit, or your inner child. In the "Owning my Own Journey" chapter, I've mentioned how difficult it is to hear our inner voice because many of us were trained to ignore it and listen to the expectations and desires of others or societal norms instead.

A personal example of this is how long it took me to realize that I didn't want to become a pharmacist. I had created an identity where I found value in appeasing my parents and receiving their affirmation. So I took on their dream of me becoming a pharmacist. But it wasn't until after my undergraduate years, plus a couple years after that, that I discovered I was on the wrong path.

A more recent example happened a few years ago when I started to understand my gift and niche in the psychology and practice of Leadership and Culture. The thought of getting my Ph.D. in Leadership piqued my interest. Perhaps I could finally be the doctor I had once that I would be. I looked up programs and even met with a counselor and spoke to my leader at work about it. I then took time to pray and reflect, as I knew that deciding to do this program would be a family effort of balancing work and kids.

This time, it was easier and quicker since I had practiced quieting my mind and hearing my inner voice. What I heard were questions about why I wanted the doctorate: Would getting the doctorate truly help me make the impact in the world I wanted to make? Or was it my Human desire to achieve my doctorate degree and receive affirmation from my parents and society for having a Ph.D. title? I also heard my inner wisdom telling me I was afraid to pursue my purpose. What if I fail? What if no one likes what I have to say? A doctorate would surely make it easier for people to see me as credible in Leadership and Culture and then be open to my insights. But then all the leaders in the coaching and culture space who didn't have degrees, but had extensive practice and experience, came to mind. If they could do it without credentials, surely I could, too. So I decided to use my energy to do more Leadership and Culture work instead of going back to school.

One way to prompt your inner voice so that you can practice hearing it again is to throw yourself into new situations. The discomfort will trigger the voices you have to surface, allowing you to practice deciphering which voice is truly yours. An example of how you can do this in your career is to switch up roles every two to three years. Additionally, if you are not at the point where your current position fulfills your life purpose and brings you joy, you can switch companies to further push yourself out of your comfort zone.

Your Divine Past and Present

If you feel stagnant or stuck right now, have 100% peace knowing you are exactly where you are meant to be and that your past and present are how you unlock your future. For example, when I became curious about the possibility of a career other than pharmacy, a big fear in switching career paths was that I would waste the years of experience and knowledge I had gained in the pharmaceutical industry. To my surprise, however, my next step of pivoting into leadership was due to my pharmacy training. I was able to learn and practice a new skill set while leveraging my prior pharmacy experience.

Another instance is my current role as Chief Purpose and Operating Officer for The Multifamily Mindset. For over a decade, I thought I would retire with my prior company as a Head of Human Resources. The cost to switch seemed incredibly large as my whole career was centered around HR, pharmacy, and retail operations. However, my prior roles and experience in Training and Development and Talent Management truly set me up to lead a company whose primary offering is development curriculum.

Your past and present are full of insights, lessons, and experiences that were sent to grow you so that WHEN you decide to chase your purpose, you will still have every tool, skill, and resource you might need to take each next step.

Chapter 15

Self-Actualization and Purpose

In Maslow's "A Theory of Motivation," he explains you do not need to master each level to access the next. This means you also do not have to master Esteem, Career, and Achievement to access the highest level and end goal, which is Self-Actualization and Purpose.

Self-actualization is about identity. It is about finding and knowing who you are as Spirit and the talents you have been uniquely and intentionally blessed with for your mission. Purpose is discovering with clarity the specific impact - the exact change - you were meant to make in this world.

But don't mistake *accessing* the Self-Actualization and Purpose level for *attaining* or *mastering* self-actualization and purpose because they are far from the same thing. Accessing this level means there are moments in your life where you feel connected to your authentic Spirit self and create from that state for the good of others. Attaining or mastering the level means you are ready to Unbecome at any moment. It means you are actively and intentionally being aware of, resisting the temptation to act in, and transcending above your Human ego so that you can stay in your Spirit state and act in full accordance with love, abundance, joy, peace, and more.

Maslow estimated that only 2% of people can reach the state of self-actualization (Innobatics, n.d.). Many think they are self-actualizing but have only begun to understand what it takes to do so. Additionally, I've learned that a true understanding of self-love and being aware and willing to explore that fully within yourself is required to reach your whole purpose. An authentic understanding reveals your dual nature and your power as Spirit in Human form.

Remember, purpose begins with our relationship with God. Because our ultimate purpose lies in the plans He has for our lives, enabled by the unique and powerful gifts He masterfully and intentionally gives us.

> *"Each of you should use whatever gift you have received to serve others, as faithful stewards of God's grace in its various forms."*
>
> —1 Peter 4:10 (NIV)

I have come to witness that every person is born with a unique purpose in life. I believe that our Spirit selves already know our life's purpose at birth and that we still have access to that insight. The problem is that we have been trained to listen and follow other people's expectations of us and our future so regularly that we forget how to listen to our inner voice and wisdom. Referring back to when our brains transition from delta to theta frequencies, we lose touch with our connection to God within us, which is our authentic Spirit or child-like selves. I believe we were each born with a unique purpose - a specific way to help others through this world. And it is through self-transforming up Maslow's hierarchy that we are given opportunities to discover and strengthen our God-given talents and abilities, which are masterfully designed and assigned to help us execute our purpose. When I finally found my life purpose, I looked back at the long, zig-zag process it took for me to figure out what that purpose was. I wanted to streamline it to see how I might help someone else replicate that process for themselves.

One of the ways to discover where you are meant to go is to consider what you recall from your childhood because our inner child, the Spirit we were before this world got ahold of us, is inside us still. And it knows our destiny and can guide us.

Here are a series of questions to help you look into your past, see yourself as a child, and look for facts, feelings, and details you may have missed in those moments but may be able to perceive now as an observer. The answers are hints and clues that you can put together to lead you to your purpose. Reflect upon and answer the following questions to see if they help you discover or unlock hints that move you closer to your Life Purpose. Take your time with this exercise. Carve out a day or two or space these questions out over a week to allow yourself time to look into your childhood and find the correct answer.

- What is my dream job?
  This could be a novel job or a mix of current roles. If you're not clear yet on this answer, try these alternate "dream job" questions:
  What level do I see myself operating at?
  What function do I see myself performing?
  What specific project/change would I love to lead for a company?
- If I had all the time and money I needed to be comfortable, what kind of work would I do?
- What volunteer work would I gladly sign up for if I am available to do so this weekend?
- What did I want to be as a young child? What about that role excited me, and why?
- What's my passion? Suppose I am exhausted at the end of the week. What is a work task or activity I would be able to immediately find the energy to do and get excited about it?
- What are my signature strengths?
  If needed, you can take a strengths assessment to help you figure this out. Marcus Buckingham's *StandOut Assessment*, the *DISC Assessment*, *StrengthsFinder 2.0, and/or Enneagram* are a few options.
- What tasks or skills are easier for me to do than others, even if I don't enjoy doing them?

- What kinds of shows easily capture my attention, keep me intrigued, and why?
- What kinds of problems am I really good at solving?
- If you could find out what other people you've worked with think about you, what are the three things you'd want them to say?

Next, pair the answers to the questions above with the answers to this next set of questions.

- What do you quickly wake up for that excites you without hesitation?
- What key experiences have you had?

If it helps you to better see what this discovery looks like, here is what I saw and learned about my own talents and abilities:

- When I was young, I had a great memory, which helped me learn quickly and be a good test taker. As I got older, I realized in addition to retaining a lot of the information I had learned, I didn't compartmentalize it. My brain combined all I had learned over time, and I could call on insights from one topic and apply them directly to other topics. For example, learning the taxonomy code in elementary school exposed me to Latin. That made it easier for me to process other concepts. Understanding Latin also helped me later in college, especially when learning anatomy and diseases in my physiology and infectious diseases courses. As a business leader, this talent also allows me to connect short-term actions to long-term strategies and outcomes.
- I am blessed with a high emotional intelligence. When I was younger, it showed up as empathy and thoughtfulness for others. As I got older, it helped me accurately read people's energy, emotions, and unstated concerns and build meaningful connections with strangers.
- As a child and still as an adult, I thoroughly enjoy watching lawyer and detective shows like "Monk," "The Mentalist," "The Good

Wife," and "Criminal Minds," as well as shows that make you think like "House" and "This Is Us." I learned that I am drawn to these kinds of shows because they demonstrate how specific events motivate people, causing them to act or react intellectually, which both stimulates and intrigues me. In the last decade, I've also been able to grow my gift of identifying patterns in behavior. Specifically, I observe a person's words and actions for consistency or lack thereof, create an identity and belief profile from that data, and then tease out the rules they operate off of so I can anticipate their next action. Applying this skill to my work helped me discover my effectiveness at coaching and developing leaders and transforming organizational cultures, both of which ignited and refueled me.

Our purpose is specific, clear, and unique. It doesn't change; it fine-tunes, especially as we grow stronger in Spirit. However, how we take action on our purpose can shift. For example, I had thought that my ultimate mission was to be a Chief Human Resources Officer for a Fortune organization. But, I discovered that my vision had evolved to Head of Talent Management and then to Chief Culture Officer.

Additionally, I had always seen myself as a business leader first and HR professional second. Plus, I was always interested in stepping out of the key support role and stepping into Operations as the Business Leader. One day, after chatting with a close friend and mentor about the Chief Culture Officer (CPO) role within my organization, she replied back with a new C-Suite role called the Chief Purpose Officer. I hadn't heard of it before, but learning more about it resonated with who I am and the change I wish to see in the world: that we could individually and collectively live for a purpose more than profit. I choose to believe the interest I've had in business and leadership since I was a child, all the learning opportunities I've had, and the conversation with my friend about a CPO, were divine signals and omens that I was open to. And putting them together helped me identify and create my current reality, serving as Chief Purpose and Operating Officer.

No experience is wasted. Every scenario, good, bad, or indifferent, is intentionally sent to help us discover our God-given abilities, Spirit identity, and life purpose. Think of life as the ultimate scavenger hunt! Stay open to the lessons, clues, and connections that are embedded in your everyday life. If you focus your brain on seeing these hints, you will start to find them.

Writing Down Your Purpose

When you discover your purpose, it will likely come to you as a vision or impression. It may also come to you as part of a picture or as a fully descriptive one. When you find these revelations, write them down so you can be clear on what is needed to take ACTION.

Getting clarity for yourself may take time. Start by writing down what you think your Life Purpose is. Create iterations until the words embody emotion and reflect who you are and what you stand for. If you command your brain and Spirit to seek your purpose and focus energy on it, I am confident you will find it. Here are the iterations I have had for my Life's Purpose:

1. To help people grow and develop.
2. To coach people to become their best selves.
3. To help others find their God-given abilities and Life Purpose.
4. To help others connect to their Spirit-self.
5. To help others change their Life's Question from "What am I getting?" to "Who am I becoming?"
6. To change the world by transforming their Life's Question from "What am I getting?" to "Who am I becoming?"

Your Life Purpose doesn't need to sound or look good. It doesn't need to make sense to anyone else but you. It does, however, need to inspire you, fill you with emotion, and move you to take immediate action.

I believe we were all given a destiny to pursue that can meaningfully change the world. Whether we choose to follow it or not is 100% of our choice. God and His messengers will send signs to help prompt and guide us. At the beginning of my spiritual journey, I had many doubts where I felt unsure of myself and unworthy, so I never took ACTION.

And I'm certain there were other signs I missed altogether. Now that I am closer to God and familiar with His love and power, it is easier to perceive when He is at work in my life. I can feel my inner Spirit cueing me to pay attention to clues - certain events, persons, ideas, numbers - so that I can figure out what each clue means and discover what my next ACTION needs to be.

Know this, if you are brave enough to follow the dreams that God has placed in your heart, He will provide and supply whatever you may need all along the way. This assistance may or may not come packaged exactly as you have asked, but God has great wisdom, and He provides that wisdom to us. We must trust His way is greater than our own and choose that path of self-discovery. I believe God, Jesus, and the Holy Spirit are in each of us, as well as the Angels, Archangels, our Ancestors, and all the forces for good in the universe that stand ready to assist us. Once we realize that, we can tap into that power with steps of faith and move forward to achieve our dreams.

You know you've found your Life Purpose when it scares you. After all, passion IS literally sacrifice, not a fun hobby or pastime. It is scary to "pick up your cross" and pursue your purpose. It demands conviction and faith in the face of some of the most trying challenges you'll ever encounter. As you forge ahead, remember the declaration in 2 Timothy 1:7 (New King James Version [NKJV]), "For God did not give you a spirit of fear, but of power and love and self-control."

The Meaning of Life

Now that you've made it this far in your journey to Unbecome, at some point, you may be asking yourself, what is all of this for? What is the meaning of life? As preposterous or boastful as this may sound, I am convinced I have the correct answer. Based on my experiences to date, I have come to understand that the meaning of life is **to seek God,** and we do this by discovering our true nature as Spirit and using our talents to fulfill our life purpose.

As Spirits in Human form, we have the ability to create ANYTHING we can dream up or imagine. The greatest reward and joy comes from activating our faith by dreaming big and creating the desires of our heart. The first time we create something that we once thought was impossible is both energizing and empowering. We can also take the power that God has given us and dream one level higher by using our creative power for the good of others. And I stress for the good of others because this creative power and ability can be equally applicable for selfish or destructive reasons.

Marilyn Monroe said, "The sky is not the limit. Your mind is." So, in the same way that God declared, "Let there be light" (Genesis 1:3 [NIV]) and created the world he imagined, "Let" yourself do the same. Let your Unbecome-d, child-like self dream and believe again. Unleash your faith and imagination. Love yourself enough to see the possibility and power God has given you. You will be floored with awe, wonder, and divine joy when you do. Experiencing life this way, which IS what it means to act in Spirit, IS what life is all about.

Our Creative Power as Spirit

Many successful people will say, "I'm nothing special. If I can do it, so can you." The latter part of that is true, but I disagree with the beginning. Every person on this Earth is special. Actually, we are all extraordinary. Each person has a powerful Spirit living inside of them that is impatiently waiting to be unleashed. That impatience shows up as feeling unsettled with your current situation or just feeling like there should be "more," even if you don't know what that "more" is for yourself just yet.

We are made in the image and likeness of God. To me, this does not necessarily mean that we look like Him. It means He gave us His power to create so we might co-create this world with Him. Those who state they are not spiritual or practice faith may refer to this creative power as manifestation. Regardless of how or if you associate with a faith-filled background, I promise you, you have this power too. And when you find the courage to discover it, it will leave you in unfathomable levels of awe, wonder, and gratitude.

Every human, whether with pure or faulty intent, has access to this power. Therefore, it becomes easy to forget that this power comes from

God. When we can stay mindful that our power comes from a higher source and that it was given to us to create specific things in the world for the greater good of all, then we can experience the highest level of self-actualization and purpose. When we co-create with God and the spiritual realm, our ability to perceive that creation is amplified in its speed, size, and impact. Two is always better than one, and everything is possible when we are able to activate and partner with the spiritual realm.

> *"Your gift will make room for you, and puts you in the presence of great things."*
>
> *—Steve Harvey*

Personally, I saw this shift happen to me in 2016. Up until then, there were achievements I had that I now know, in retrospect, were rooted in Esteem, Career, and Achievement. I did not fully understand how God was helping to elevate me. I took all the credit and, therefore, also endured all the weight. These achievements included:

- Getting hired by a national Retailer as a Pharmacy Technician
- Getting bartending and waitressing jobs to help pay off $30,000+ in debt
- Getting out of debt and starting to have enough money to pay my bills on time and save for the future
- Being promoted to a Pharmacy Trainer from my previous role as a Pharmacy Technician

Also, getting serious about my relationship with my husband and challenging myself to grow in Love for the simple reason of becoming more like God is the key moment I learned how to stay in Spirit while in Human form. Since then, I've been able to activate this power by bringing God into my goals and giving Him all the credit so that I could also give Him the burdens of my human desires and focus on courageously and joyfully creating the life of my dreams. I fine-tuned this ability through practice. Practice is facing internal battles head-on that arise from setting and conquering goals. You'll find my goals listed below. And even though they may look different from yours, the internal battles are universal because they center around choosing our Spirit over our Human selves.

These goals included:

- Switching my career path from Pharmacist to Business Leader
- Getting accepted by and graduating from an MBA program with Honors
- Obtaining scholarships for my MBA program
- Elevating to a Training Manager
- Moving to New England and landing a promotion after graduate school
- Marrying my perfect match
- Relocating to California with my company
- Becoming a Mom to my first son
- Transitioning into residential real estate
- Becoming a Mom to my second son
- Elevating to an Executive Director Role in a Fortune 5 Company
- Expanding my career to include multifamily real estate
- Being selected to lead company-wide leadership and culture initiatives
- Serving as a Chief Purpose and Operating Officer
- Closing our first multifamily deal as a General Partner
- Writing and finishing this book
- Creating my ideal quality of life daily
- Having Absolute Financial Freedom

Impact Versus Achievement

This is one of the biggest nuggets of wisdom I can share. Again, as I covered in the Duality grid, Impact is of the Spirit, while Achievement is of the Human condition. These two distinctions are about the main intent in your heart when you set and pursue any goal. At the bottom of Maslow's Pyramid, the main intention of our physiological needs is primarily human survival. There may be additional motivating factors that are selfless, but the most significant driving factor is our needs.

But as we elevate up the pyramid, we find that our motivating factors become less about ourselves and more about others. For example, I want financial safety so that my family doesn't have to worry anymore about being unable to pay bills. Or, I want to bridge my relationship with my ex-wife so that my kids don't have to suffer through our disagreements. I also want to get that promotion so I can make a difference for the team I would lead.

It is at the self-actualization and purpose level that we make a transformational shift from our primary motivator of being ourselves and asking, "What can we get from a situation?" to our primary motivator of being and wondering, "Who am I becoming for others and the greater good of the world?" It is at this pivotal transition when we can consciously and intentionally become aware of and kill our egos at any given moment and sacrifice our Human wants and desires for what is good and best for others.

The tricky part about making this transition is that most people are blind to the fact that their primary motivating factor is their desire to say they attained the next level of "success" to appease their Human need to feel valued or important. This self-focused, extrinsic motivation influences how they go about accomplishing their goal. There is a tendency to micromanage, move quicker than others are able to follow, and keep focused on the goal itself rather than the identity transformation one must go through to attract and obtain that goal.

This focus on impact and serving others over what you can get or achieve brings to mind the story of Kanaka Wai Wai. Kanaka Wai Wai was a wealthy man who longed to be with God in Heaven and gain eternal life. However, he loved his earthly riches more than God. Many can look with judgment on Kanaka Wai Wai and wonder, "How foolish he is to choose earthly riches over God?" Yet, the hard truth is that most of the world makes the same choice every single day.

Iesu Me Ke Kanaka Waiwai (Jesus and The Rich Man) - music by John K. Almeida[8]
First recorded in 1946 by John Almeida with the Genoa Keawe trio.

Ma ke alahele 'o Iesû	Along the road, Jesus
I hālāwai aku ai	Met
Me ke kanaka 'ōpio hanohano	With a distinguished young man
Kaulana i ka waiwai	Who was known for his wealth
Pane mai e ka 'ōpio	The young man said,
'E ku'u Haku maika'i	"My good lord,
He aha ho'i ka'u e hana aku ai	What must I do
I loa'a e ke ola mau?	To gain eternal life?"
Hui:	Chorus:
E hā'awi, e hā'awi lilo	"Give, give away all
I kou mau waiwai	Of your possessions
Huli a hahai mai ia'u	Then come and follow me
I loa'a e ke ola mau ia 'oe	In order to gain eternal life"
Minamina e ka 'ōpio	The young man grieved
I kona mau waiwai	Over his wealth
I ke kū'ai a hā'awi lilo aku	Unwilling to sell and give all
I ka po'e nele a hune	To the poor and destitute
Huli a'e 'o Iesū lā	Jesus then turned
Pane aku i ka 'ōpio	And answered the man,
'A'ole a'e hiki ke kanaka waiwai	"Rich man, you will not enter
I ke aupuni o ka lani	The Kingdom of Heaven

---

8 Source: Keola Donaghy, Copyright J. Almeida 1971, Translated by Haunani Bernardino - Based on the parable from Matthew 19:16-24, Almeida composed the music in 1915, for a Mormon Church in Honolulu who rejected the song because it sounded too much like a hula. The original chords and music was not the way it is sung today.

Now, this tale can be interpreted in many different ways. However, what I see in this parable is that Jesus is not asking us to live with nothing and also be poor and destitute. I believe He is asking us to be willing to give it all away to "come follow me" and pursue the mission He has assigned to each of us, just like He did. When we have a clear vision for ourselves and the world, how willing are we to risk it all to bring this vision to life? Or do we stall and pause pursuing our Life Purpose because of worry and concern around earthly riches?

Often many are not willing to relinquish the comforts of the flesh for the chance to attain this state of Nirvana or Heaven on Earth. Only when we put our faith in action and remain focused on our missions can we experience eternal life, which is an abundance in every capacity and greater than we can imagine or comprehend.

> *"Service... using whatever it is you produce your product as a way of giving back to the world. When you shift the paradigm of whatever it is you choose to do to service and you bring significance to that, success, I promise you, will follow you. Service and Significance equals Success."*
>
> —Oprah Winfrey

My Great Leap Towards Self-Actualization and Purpose

July 1, 2022, is the day I finally found the courage to step fully into my purpose and self-actualize. I decided to leave the company I "grew up" in and loved dearly because who I was and who I strived to be no longer aligned with the company's identity, beliefs, and values. I had not been fulfilled for a while but stayed for multiple reasons. Those reasons included fear of the unknown and starting all over again, along with the fear of giving up what I already had: perceived income security, strong friendships that I had made, and a sense of status from my role and title. But once I decided to resign, it became crystal clear to me that the only person to blame for my lack of fulfillment was myself. It was hard to accept the truth, but it was the truth nevertheless. I stayed and endured an unhealthy work-life balance, leaders, and a culture longer than I should have because I valued the money, security, and status that came with leading a Fortune organization more than I valued my quality of life and peace of mind.

I saw an anonymous quote a while back that struck me. It read something like this: *"Your Salary is the bribe they give you to stop chasing your dreams."* Those who worked with me would say I was one of the most conscious leaders they've known. Yet still, I felt that I had blindly sold my soul.

Taking back control of my life and daring to choose what God was calling me to do instead of what this world or my ego was telling me to do, was the most freeing and empowering moment I have ever felt. I can't remember the last time I felt that ALIVE and LIMITLESS, where the world was safe, life was fun, and I had the power to create whatever was in my heart. The last time I experienced that feeling had to have been when I was a very young child when I still operated in my Spirit state and was entirely Unbecome.

> "There is freedom waiting for you...And you ask, 'What if I fall?'
> Oh, but my darling, What if you fly?"
>
> - Erin Hanson

Unbecoming

We are human and are easily tempted to operate in our Human state. Unbecoming is a conscious effort to be mindful of which identity you're operating in and choose intentionally and consciously towards your ideal life experience rather than run on autopilot from your past.

Unbecoming isn't a one-time event; it is an ongoing practice you can implement each time you choose to evolve or grow in an aspect of your life and find yourself stalled or stuck in the process. They say the journey IS the destination, and I see Unbecoming as the journey within. As you practice and master the differences between Becoming, Unbecoming and Being, you will gain a better understanding of who you are as Spirit. And when you can truly identify as Spirit first, you will also find and know God and gain self-love, clarity, peace, joy, and abundance, no matter what this world throws your way.

Our Deepest Fear

Our deepest fear is not that we are inadequate.
Our deepest fear is that we are powerful beyond measure.
It is our light, not our darkness that most frightens us.
We ask ourselves, who am I to be brilliant, gorgeous, talented and fabulous?
Actually, who are you not to be?
You are a child of God.
Your playing small does not serve the world.
There's nothing enlightened about shrinking so that other people won't feel insecure around you.
We are all meant to shine, as children do.
We were born to make manifest the glory of God that is within us.
It's not just in some of us; it's in everyone.
And as we let our own light shine, we unconsciously give other people permission to do the same.
As we are liberated from our own fear, our presence automatically liberates others.
—Marianne Williamson

"When I stand before God at the end of my life, I would hope to be able to say, "I used everything you gave me."
—*Erma Bombeck*

Letter to My Loved Ones

My Beloved Tribe,

I hope you come to understand we are Spirits in Human form so that you can free yourselves from suffering in this life and unlock the abundance God desires for each of us.

It is a great temptation we all face to waste this life experience by being distracted. Let's have the time of our lives knowing that when God created us, He designed each of us with a purpose, a unique way to co-create with Him…to bring Heaven to earth…to change the world in a powerful and special way.

It can seem hazy and unclear how we go about doing this. It can be hard to see what the first step may be for you. Draw closer to Him and focus on loving others; I promise you, you'll figure it out. In due time, if your intent is pure in seeking Him and you are open to the ways of the Spirit, you will perceive the signals and omens sent to you.

Don't get so preoccupied with worry, stress, guilt, or shame that you forget to enjoy everyday MIRACLES, like getting to wake up and breathe, and see, and hear, and hold loved ones in physical form. Prioritize reconnecting with your child-like self and find the courage to live from that space of possibility, awe, and wonder.

Don't get so distressed by money, power, and popularity that you forget your ultimate goal in this life is to grow in Love, which is God. Trust that Love heals and then go be a source of Love for others because this world has so much healing to do.

Don't get too much in your head about shoulda, coulda, woulda, what if, or maybe that you forget to LIVE and LIVE RIGHT NOW! Living isn't about acquiring everything you ever dreamed of. Living is about being present and letting yourself be yourself and not who others want you to be. Living is enjoying each moment as you experience it and being brave enough to take action toward your dreams in spite of your current circumstances.

Your deepest and greatest dreams are in your heart because God put them there. And because they are from God, every single one of those goals is yours for the taking when you are open to God's way and you want them bad enough to take action on them. I pray you truly grasp the LIMITLESS power you have as Spirit. I pray that as you grow stronger in your power, you remember who you are as Spirit so that you create with pure intent for the good of others.

I believe God, Jesus, the Holy Spirit within you, the angels, Archangels, our ancestors, and all the forces for good in the universe are here and ever-present to assist you in creating everything you can imagine for God's glory.

Matthew 5:14-16 (NIV) says, "You are the light of the world...let your light shine before others, so that they may see your good works and give glory to your Father who is in heaven."

Namaste,
    -RLT

Further Practice

The intended audience for this and the next section is your Spirit self. The following content will resonate with it. If you feel triggered or confused, that may be a sign that your Human self is dominant at the moment. I believe simply reading this imparts a self-accountability towards doing good and being the most outstanding leader you can be for God, yourself, and others in all facets of your life.

There are also two words I'd like to highlight to tee up these chapters - Disciple and Prophet.

A disciple is a student, learner, or follower. We are all born disciples; at the beginning of our lives, we don't get to choose who or what we are disciples of. As we covered at the beginning of the book, we absorb, learn and follow our environment even before we are born. As we age, we gain the ability to choose what and who we are disciples of and, more powerfully, become a prophet. However, we do not always choose to exercise our power because doing so means forgetting our Human condition and activating our Spirit identity.

Regarding Prophets, when I was younger, I learned that only certain people were chosen to be prophets and that all the prophets this world would ever see have already come and gone. However, through my experience and learning about others' experiences, I have come to understand that this is not the case at all. A Prophet is someone who teaches others the wisdom they have gained from their experiences and helps lead them through similar challenges.

I believe **we are all Prophets**. We are each uniquely called to share our transformation stories and to teach others a way to go from hopelessness to power, from partial truths to the whole truth, from pain to love, from fear to faith, and from nothing to abundance. There is no story too small or insignificant; there is always at least one person out there that can benefit from our story should we have the courage to share it. This world has done a masterful job training us to believe in our limited Human condition, so much so that we don't share our wisdom and stories with each other and prevent meaningful connection and necessary healing from occurring.

Intentionally shifting from disciple to Prophet is a huge deal. It means you understand how to operate from subconscious to conscious. It means you've experienced how to use your divine power to act and stay in spirit. It means you are capable of being purpose-driven.

On the next page are several concepts and tactics that assist me in maintaining my Unbecoming, and I share them with you in the chance they help you, too. If you read this skeptically and think these tactics won't work for you, that's fine. But what if they do? Would you rather stay where you are and blend with the crowd than be different and live the life God dreamed for you?

Change

Please take a moment to reflect on or journal about the following question:
- What changes do you not want to happen in your life and why?

Most people avoid or resist change because our brains register it as a lack of safety. But, the problem is that change is inevitable and continuous, so having a change-averse mindset creates a perpetual state of feeling unsafe and stressed. So, to counter that resistance, allow yourself to now reflect on or journal about this next question:
- What are some changes you want to happen in your life?

If you could even list one thing in your answer, then it is not change you do not like, but the perspective you take on the situation and the meaning you give to steer clear of it. For instance, a breakup for one person can be a sad thing they want to avoid, while the same breakup for another can be a positive thing. Relocating out of state for a new job is an amazing opportunity for a parent, but it may feel catastrophic for their high school kid who has to now leave their girlfriend or boyfriend and friends. No one situation is inherently good or bad; it just is. But it is we, as masterful storytellers, who add our perspective and meaning to it.

While change can be uncomfortable and uncertain, it is the gateway to growth. So it's essential we find a way to reframe change when it happens so that we feel safe and empowered.

Most prayers are about asking God to change our situation, change our problems or change other people. I've found success in transforming my prayer life and asking God to change me instead. I've shared specific examples in my stories and testimonies of how I've applied that prayer to my transformation up Maslow's Hierarchy of Needs pyramid. This is not easy, and many of us will initially feel unwilling to be inconvenienced. But once we get past that feeling and embrace the continued journey for change, we find ourselves willing to unravel and Unbecome again and again and persevere in our desire to be our Spirit self.

Your Environment

"You are the average of the five people you spend the most time with."

-Jim Rohn

Whether we love it or not, we are a product of who we spend the most time with. For most adults, we have the power to control this aspect of our lives. Yet, we don't exercise it because we are not always aware of how others negatively impact our thinking and energy. And it isn't always easy to switch up social circles.

Seek out friends and mentors who are going where you want to go and living the way you want to live. You can find these partners at work events, community events, development seminars, networking conferences, and even at the grocery store. Put yourself out there and discover those around you. There is likely at least one person in your life that encourages and inspires you if you make it a point to seek that person out. Another powerful tool I use, if I'm not able to physically get around like-Spirited individuals, is the internet and social media, either directly or by simply watching content that feeds my spirit instead of destroying or distracting it.

> *"Proximity is power. If you can get proximity with people that are the best in the world, things can happen because of all of the people they know, the insights they have and the life experience they have. They can save you a decade of time by one insight."*
>
> -Tony Robbins

Mastering Our Minds

> *"Do not be conformed to this world, but be transformed by the renewal of your mind, that by testing you may discern what is the will of God, what is good and acceptable and perfect."*
>
> -Romans 12:2 (NKJV)

I discussed earlier the role of our brains in Unbecoming. Mastering our Minds IS the key to accessing our Spirit. Even when you Unbecome, there will be continued distractions to keep you stalled on your life path. IGNORE THEM. Every upset you encounter is a distraction sent to take energy away from your purpose. Distractions, often showing up as inconveniences, upsets, challenges, or barriers, keep us from being able to BE.

But, we CAN just BE. When we invite children to play pretend, they have no problem being anything they can imagine and can do so in a split second. No resources, no problem. They find whatever they have, see it through the eyes of possibility and creativity, and can turn a broom into a firehouse, a piece of cloth into a cape, or a toy block into a cupcake. Those who have experienced being able to see with possibility understand how they can see a way when they thought there wasn't one.

At the core of mastering your mind is the ability to control your inner dialogue, which runs practically non-stop every day. We constantly absorb material and messages, and what we believe is a byproduct of the repeating messages we let into our bodies. Here are several ways to take back control of the quality of your inner dialogue so that you can master your mind:

- **Music** - listen to music that makes you move and has lyrics aligned with what you want to believe or embody. When music inspires you to move, you more readily absorb the energy and messages carried in the song.
- **Motivational talks, podcasts, and sermons** - having them play in the background in the house or the car helps to fill in brain space that would usually be taken up by historically negative inner dialogue. For example, listening to motivational series can fill up the space if you're normally a worrier and easily find things to worry about. You are now replacing worry with affirmations.
- **Reminders around your home or workspace** - It's easy to fall into a Human way of thinking throughout the day. Posting reminders of your goals, hopes, and dreams throughout the house or in your car can create an opportunity for you to pause, reflect on how you're operating, and reset, if needed.
- **Heated Yoga and Meditation** - Yoga, in general, is beneficial. Still, I find that heated yoga better helps me with mastering my mind. The heat helps my body warm up quickly and hastens my being in a state of flow. Also, the heat easily triggers my Human flight or fight response in my brain, which provides me more opportunities to practice taming and quieting my mind. This is meditation. When I begin, I am strictly in a Human state where I focus mainly on the condition of my body and how it feels. So my thoughts are: "I am getting hot." "How much longer do I have in this class?" "This is so hard." "I can't last this long." For me, yoga begins when I become aware of my Human state and challenge myself to switch my focus from the physical discomfort of having my brain and body at odds with one another and in two different places to being one; thus bringing my mind back to the present moment where I can control my breathe and enjoy each moment instead of wishing it was over. Through this practice, you can learn to be comfortable and mindful in uncomfortable or stressful situations.
- **Ujjayi breathing** - Ujjayi breathing is a technique that focuses on breathing through your nose while compressing your throat.

The narrowed vocal cords create a rushing or hissing sound, very similar to Darth Vader's breathing. The benefits of Ujjayi are numerous: it soothes the nervous system, calms the mind, and increases psychic sensitivity. It relieves insomnia, slows heart rate, and lowers blood pressure (Himalayan Yoga Institute, n.d.). I practice Ujjayi breathing whenever I find myself mentally or physically stressed and need to calm down. It is also a powerful tactic to stay calm and present during yoga or exercise.

- **Forcing ourselves to take action** - Nothing helps you get out of your own head like using that energy to take action. I am not saying to stop ever contemplating a decision. I'm saying don't fall into "analysis paralysis." Take the two or three options you are considering, make a quick list of the pros and cons of each, then choose the most favorable based on the data you've come up with. Come up with a first step toward the option you picked. Next, as Nike commands, "Just Do It!" This is a 15-minute exercise MAX. Stop overthinking. Taking action sooner will give you practice in trusting yourself to briefly pause and pivot when you experience a stall or delay.
- **Gratitude** - I advocate daily gratitude discipline and suggest you do the same. Every day, wake up and go to bed, identifying things to be grateful for. Really get lost in your gratitude and feel the joy, love, and abundance that comes with it. In my personal growth in gratitude, I found that, at first, it was hard to find many things to be grateful for. Then, it became easier for me. Eventually, I even found small miracles in my every day. Now, my heart has evolved to where I have full gratitude for every challenge I encounter in life.
- **Wise Counsel** - Albert Einstein said, "We can not solve our problems with the same level of thinking that created them." There are two ways to elevate the level of your thinking. The first way is to discover what identity or belief allowed the problem to occur or perpetuate in the first place. The second way is to solicit people with the same problem as you, even if they have different backgrounds or life experiences. However, I do suggest that you

find others with similar values. This could be someone you know, like a loved one or friend. It could also be an acquaintance or someone that you look up to or can feel safe with, like a coach, mentor, or therapist. Having a different perspective is invaluable because the answer to all the problems we face, especially when we are stuck, can exist where we are not looking. So we need others who can see the other 10,999,950 bits of information a second that you can't consciously process to gain a broader, more complete perspective of the problem AND the possibilities that can connect with it.

- **Create and perform personal mantras** - Our internal voice that repeats over and over again throughout the day is mighty in our brain's programming. However, what is more powerful is our "out loud" voice. Our brains stand at attention and listen whenever it hears us speak. Therefore, it is helpful to not only think affirmative things but to also perform them as a mantra out loud with full expression on your face and body. The more emotionally charged you are when saying these affirmations, the more likely your brain believes them to be true. Here are some affirmations or declarations I've vocalized for myself over the years. You can make your own, borrow, or fine-tune one of these. Choose the ones you feel bring you the most power.

- I am courageous.
- I am disciplined.
- I am consistent.
- I am persistent.
- I am fully equipped.
- I am magnetic.
- I am divinely protected.
- I am exactly where I'm meant to be.
- I am right on time.
- I have an excessive amount of time.
- I am the MASTER of my mind, body, and spirit.

- I am blessed and highly favored.
- I am smart.
- I am beautiful.
- I am talented.
- I am generous.
- I have more than enough.
- I eat and live to increase the life in me so that I may give life to and heal others.
- I am God's daughter and one of His greatest warriors of all time.
- I am present and alive.

In addition to saying your affirmations out loud, it can also help to create new ones. Here are some steps and reflection questions you can use when writing custom affirmations. Select a few that resonate with you, and once created, recite them out loud.

- When thinking about your current affirmations, did any of them feel weird to say or trigger imposter syndrome for you? Did you speak some louder than others?
- Which ones did you say with full energy, conviction, and with your entire being?
- Which ones did you say with hesitation or doubt? How can you change or make adjustments to those?
- Pick the most important mantra to you and reflect on your reaction when you say it out loud. Anytime you don't feel authentic or true, that's an indicator you don't believe it about yourself. Keep saying it out loud each day until you start to believe it. The more animated and emotional you get when performing it, the quicker you become it.

Control

One of the biggest truths I've discovered revolves around our ability to have control and use it. I used to believe that there are three buckets of control: 1) things we can't control, 2) things we can control, and 3) things we can partially control, or in other words, influence. However, through a lot of life experience, I understand clearly now there are only 2 buckets: 1) the things we can control and 2) the things we can influence.

First and foremost, the only thing we can truly control is ourselves. However, everything else falls under our influence. I imagine someone might ask, "Well what about the weather, Rowen?" To that, I respond, "Global Warming." The problem in our thinking is that we have an expectation of what our journey should look like. We want things sooner or different than how they may be. We must realize that we are co-creators with God and all the forces for good in the Universe, so whenever we create, we must be open to the possibility that there may be a way that is greater than our own way. I find peace knowing that God has always and will always work all things together for my good.

This concept can be difficult to accept, if not intimidating. So, I challenge you to live out a week of your life knowing and expecting that you can influence everything. How will that change your action and the outcomes you can manifest or attract? How much more courageous would you be knowing you CAN make a difference with anything you choose to? You may be surprised at how holding this conviction can influence everything and reveal new solutions and actions you can take toward your goal. I encourage you to document your ideas and the mental and energetic shifts toward your Spirit self now that you can embrace this truth.

"The Brave may not live forever, but the Cautious never live at all."

-Richard Branson

Work-Life Balance

People often ask me, "Leader, Businesswoman, Wife, Mother, Daughter, Sister, Mentor, Friend - how do you do it all?" My simple answer is I don't do it all at the same time. I prioritize and do only one thing at a time. Choosing one thing permits my brain to fully focus on it and get wildly creative. It becomes my purpose while also allowing me time to concentrate on my QUALITY of life and not the quantity of it.

How do I create balance with all these roles? I live with the end in mind. This seed of wisdom, as I call it, was planted when I was in high school. I was in a class called Death and Dying and participated in an assignment where you had to plan your funeral. I did everything from costing it out to who would attend, thinking about what kind of casket I'd like, and writing my own eulogy. At that age, I thought of death as a faraway event. Now that I'm older, I understand tomorrow isn't promised and that I could easily die today.

That class taught me to ask myself this at the start of my day: "If this all ended tonight, what are the things that matter the most to me and can take care of today?" When that list started to match my regular to-do list, I not only found that I had more balance but also joy and excitement. I made that shift from existing throughout my day to really living it. It's like the example I provided earlier in the book: when you're a kid at an amusement park, and your parents say, "We're leaving in an hour," you don't take your time and overthink which ride you should go on. You just start getting on the rides you love the most and maybe even find the courage to get on the scariest one you've been putting off until the end.

Now that I've programmed myself to live in a way where I would have no regrets when I die, a new question arose when I found myself asking at the end of the day: "Was I busy, accomplished or fulfilled today?" My objective for asking this question is to feel fully present and alive in each moment that I have left in this life.

Work-life balance isn't a math or time management problem. It is an identity and belief problem. When we are not clear on who we are or what we want, we say yes to everything or to too much because we want to please others or comply with societal expectations, leaving us feeling drained, busy, and unfulfilled. Unbecoming our Spirit self helps us get crystal clear on what really matters. Who you are becomes the impression you leave on this earth and the quality of experience you create for yourself. So your focus doesn't have to remain solely on what you think is a work-life balance, but on Being. And when you can focus on Being, the rest will fall into place.

Applying Maslow's Hierarchy to Leadership

Leadership isn't about being in charge. It's about taking care of those in your charge.

-Simon Sinek

This segment isn't for all leaders. This is for leaders who have decided to be purpose-driven and fully Unbecome. Self-actualization or being purpose-driven isn't for the faint of spirit; it is the highest and greatest experience level we can reach in this life. Purpose-driven leaders MUST have the following:

1. Focus on their Human need for Self-actualization / Purpose
2. Have undergone a prior TRANSFORMATION in their life
3. Commitment to being purpose-driven
4. Willingness to always go first
5. Using vulnerability to kill their ego

Focus on their Human Need for Self-Actualization/Purpose: This means you've been able to generally meet your needs in all other buckets, and you are intentionally choosing to focus energy on self-actualization. Oxford Languages defines self-actualization as " the realization or fulfillment of one's talents and potentialities." Maslow explains it as a desire "to become everything one is capable of becoming."[9] However, I define self-actualization as the conscious effort to activate your Spirit identity and then leverage your gifts and abilities to create wildly for the good of others in your own unique way. Maslow asserts that only about 2% of the world's population ever really exists at this level (Innobatics Business and Life Growth, n.d.). That said, there are many leaders who wholeheartedly, yet still mistakenly believe they have

---

[9] Maslow, "...Human Motivation."

"mastered" this. For me, their actions and decisions consistently and/or at critical moments are the measures of truth.

Have Undergone a Prior TRANSFORMATION in their Life: A big mistake a leader can make is to try to change the people they lead. The problem is that we can't change other people. We can only change ourselves, then inspire others to do the same. We can change how we have conversations and lead to garner a different response.

Thus, a key role for leaders is helping others to self-transform personally and professionally. This role is similar to that of a life coach. As an HR professional, I know that sounds radical and risky, but here's the reality: we are people, and we can't separate our work self from our home self. So when there is a professional transformation with work, there naturally is an impact on the personal level as well.

Furthermore, you can only assist others through a transformation if you genuinely understand what it feels like. Only when you experience what it means to self-transform can you help someone else through it. Transformation is not the same as change or evolution. It is important to distinguish them. Oxford Languages online defines transformation as "a *thorough* or *dramatic* change in form or appearance... A *metamorphosis*." Think of a caterpillar that transforms into a butterfly. The caterpillar is not even recognizable. Its identity and whole being from the inside out is significantly, if not completely, different from what it used to be. I don't just mean that this would apply to a really, really difficult or trying time or a time where it felt so impossible that you could break. It also applies to little belief and mindset shifts you can't see but inform different, if not opposite, behaviors. But regardless of whatever difficulty you are experiencing, if you find a way to change your beliefs and actions, you can overcome it. This is also the kind of experience a leader needs to have undergone and be willing to share and lead his/her people.

Commitment to Being Purpose-Driven: Being purpose-driven is more than having a purpose memorized or written somewhere. Being committed to your purpose means you choose actions and decisions that reinforce that purpose, ESPECIALLY when it's hard, especially when the profit & loss statement says you can't, especially when the lawyers say you shouldn't, and especially when investors or shareholders criticize you for it. I am not saying to be careless or reckless with business moves or don't make any money. I am saying only take actions that align with your purpose. Any other action is NOT an option. I am saying put purpose, helping others, and changing the world first, and watch how that unlocks a level of inspiration, energy, and mindset to where you can build abundantly and sustainably on. 99.9% of purpose-driven businesses and leaders lack the courage to see this principle through and, thus, never experience the exponential upside to purpose.

When you commit to being purpose-driven, your direct reports will feel the change. Specifically, they will see their leader behave differently in pressured situations. They will experience what it is like to be around someone who holds spiritual versus human energy in interactions. Even if they don't fully recognize or understand the spiritual side of it, they will see their leader only make decisions and choose strategies aligned with their organization's values, and that will not only build trust and credibility, it will inspire and encourage them to live and lead the same way.

Two actions can help leaders stay purpose-driven and ensure their decisions and action are aligned with their purpose: 1) create a passive income stream for yourself so your decisions aren't swayed by your need for money, and 2) care most about what God and you think of you, instead of what people think of you. Having these rules allows you to break free mentally from the fear of not having money or losing status with your employer, peers, the general public, and more. These fears can sound like these statements: "We can't do the right thing because my boss has made up their mind that they want to do option B." "Our shareholders or board of directors won't be happy." "Our stock will go down." "We might lose customers or employees." Leaders need immense clarity and courage to act in accordance with their identity and purpose. It is our Spirit self that can provide that clarity and courage.

"Setting an example is not the main means of influencing another, it is the ONLY means."

-Albert Einstein

Reflection Question: If you're a higher-level leader, how do you feel when you're up against a decision you know is not right because it contradicts some other principle you've set prior. If you make that decision, what makes you stop trying to stick to your principles? What do you say to yourself that allows you to follow suit and let the wrong decision be made?

Being mindful of the identity and beliefs that drive your actions in these moments of conflict. They are powerful skills that you will get better at as you practice them.

Willingness to Always Go First: If you've read leadership books, you may have come across the following image or one like it. There are two different scenarios depicted. The first shows a tyrannical boss pushing his/her team to pull him/her and the business forward. The second shows a servant leader in the trenches with the team directing, guiding, and encouraging them to pull the business forward together. I have seen many leaders at all levels lose discipline around their leadership and fail to be aware of instances where they boss others around instead of leading. Purpose-driven leaders do not hesitate to roll up their sleeves and stay connected with their team and employees so they fully understand what their experience is like and how their actions and decisions, directly and indirectly, impact their experience. Being willing to go first shows those you lead that what you are asking IS possible. It helps grow your team's courage and faith, especially when the following steps are difficult.

When you have influence, remember the lesson we learned from our parents or caregivers because leading adults follow a similar dynamic. Our kids follow what we do, not what we say. Many leaders forget this key principle of human behavior and suffer in frustration when their teams don't act the way they want them to.

> *"Don't worry that children never listen to you; worry that they are always watching you."*
>
> -Robert Fulghum

Using Vulnerability to Kill their Human Ego: Said a different way, leaders must be able to stay in Spirit most of the time and be mindful of when they are being Human so they can understand and mitigate any potential unwanted impact, if any. As you lead people, it becomes critical to have rituals and protect time to nurture your mind and spirit because with power comes the devil's greater ability to attack our flesh. If we aren't mindful or intentional, the devil will be able to gain a stronghold. Thus, our spirits need constant nurturing.

---

10 *MillionaireMoti, LEADER VS BOSS*, Poster (2023).

Additionally, a loving reminder is that everyone has a unique journey custom designed for them. It is tempting to want to push transformation on others because we see the positive and good on the other side. However, only you can cause and drive your own self-transformation. To push the pace of another's growth faster than they are ready is a symptom of ego. Our role as leaders is to remain in Spirit and support them through their transformation rather than trying to control them or their process.

Applying Maslow's Hierarchy to Business Strategy

This section is for those who have done the work of applying Unbecoming and Maslow's Hierarchy of Needs to their Leadership behaviors and are ready for the challenge of expanding that intentionality to those they serve through the work they lead.

Applying Maslow's Hierarchy to Business and Organizations takes mindfulness and divine courage. It takes intentionality because it is easy to lose sight of the stated purpose of an organization as leaders and employees work towards the business goals of an organization. And it takes divine courage because most of us are unaware of our duality and authentic nature as a spirit. We are easily and oftentimes blindly tempted and swayed to prioritize and follow fear, ego, or the human desire to acquire even more than the intent to give generously for the greater good.

Economics teaches us that every business and organization must have a purpose for existing. There are generally two purposes for this: monetary and virtuous, or to use my duality terminology, Human (extrinsic) and Spirit (intrinsic). Historically, for-profit organizations primarily exist for financial gain, while non-profit organizations exist to advance the greater good. There have been some organizations over the course of time that have been able to marry both together. And in the last decade or so, it's become quite the trend for businesses to adopt this idea of being purpose-driven while embedding this purpose throughout an organization.

A 2019 study by EY Beacon Institute and Harvard Business Review revealed that 85% of executives are more likely to recommend a company with a strong purpose. I believe having a purpose that helps the greater good intrigues and attracts people because it appeals to our authentic spirit nature. The core issue in blending these two kinds of purposes is that most executives try to bring this harmony alive within their infrastructure, systems, processes, and employees, yet fail to create this harmony within themselves. They set themselves up for failure by thinking the change will happen within their organization instead of primarily within the leaders themselves. And so they fail to see this duality within themselves, remain in an achievement mindset, and are unable to fully elevate themselves and their organizations to purpose.

The state of a business or organization is a reflection of its leaders' collective beliefs and habits. You cannot be a purpose-driven organization if the leaders' #1 priority subconsciously is still the achievement or success viewed in others' eyes. To say you are purpose-driven when what drives you most are image, reputation, or profits would be inauthentic. Employees at all levels will sense it, which then translates to your customers. Playing to win (pursuing the vision for the company) and playing not to lose (caring more about how you appear or how much money you're making) are not the same thing.

I'll pause here to clarify that it is absolutely acceptable and welcome for an organization to have its purpose be altruistic in addition to what is stated as the company's primary purpose. The key is to own and be that versus pretending to be something you are not. Unfortunately, like people, companies focus only on what others are doing instead of staying focused on their unique strategy. This is a clear indicator the leaders are operating from their Human selves (achievement) and not their Spirit selves (impact).

To truly be a purpose-driven organization, you MUST ALWAYS choose your company's purpose over anything else. Period. Plain and simple. Many may think it's more complicated than that, but it isn't. There will be at least a FEW KEY TIMES as leaders we realize we can't do both - we can't always do the purpose-driven thing AND the business-savvy thing, so we MUST CHOOSE. What you choose to do in those few private and extremely critical moments will matter more than the million other culturally sound things you do in public. That choice is critical to your identity and transformation. The decisions and actions taken in these critical times inform employees and customers who the organization and its leaders are and what they believe. So when you realize that you, as the leader, must transform first, your leadership team will follow.

Protecting these types of purpose-driven decisions and actions becomes more challenging when an organization becomes larger. This is because when you add more people to the equation, it takes more resources and intentionality to ensure the leaders, systems, processes, and ecosystem are in place to reinforce the Spirit self over the Human one. So many organizations and leaders today want to do this but do not know how or are unwilling to do the hard things demanded of that identity. And to add to this difficulty, leaders will not always be able to find those willing to take these steps with them since it's something each person has to figure out on his or her own.

Great news - a purpose-driven organization is absolutely possible! And by understanding the steps needed to create, execute, and maintain a purpose-driven organization, you will be able to customize those steps for your specific business and team.

Culture is King

By stating that Culture is King, I am referring to organizational culture. Renowned business consultant Peter Drucker asserts, "Culture eats strategy for breakfast." Culture is how things get done in any group setting. Every team and organization has a culture. The key to a successful purpose-driven organization is to ensure that the culture that exists within it is, in fact, the same culture that is desired or advertised. The culture you create and perpetuate must embody your desired identity, beliefs, and actions. Simply stated, a purpose-driven organization MUST do what it says it will do to keep the trust and respect of its employees and customers.

The reason leaders don't have the culture they want is that they aren't willing to do the work or make the decisions that reinforce the desired culture. Many leaders will say that's hard to do and that you don't understand the pressures we face as a business. Actually, I push back on this because I do understand. Whether we are talking about life or business, it can feel near impossible to stand firm in the vision you have when your finances or reputation are seemingly at risk. It is easier and safer to choose fear over faith because we are programmed to do so as humans.

There is a myth that culture takes time to develop. I believe that is incorrect for two reasons. First, culture happens in every moment, with every decision and action. And second, as I shared earlier, a few key moments dictate the momentum of culture. We can use these two principles to our advantage. Cultural change CAN happen quickly if leaders are crystal clear on what is expected and disciplined enough to execute and protect it.

If you google "determinants of organizational culture," you'll quickly find several different concept models. Here are mine, as I have experienced that organizational culture is created as a result of these five elements:

1. Absolute Clarity of Desired IBAO for all Leaders and Employees
2. Aligned and Committed Leadership
3. Rituals
4. Environment
5. Reinforcement

Absolute Clarity of Desired IBAO for all Leaders and Employees

In the "Love and Belonging" chapter, I introduced a concept called IBAO, which stands for Identity + Beliefs → Determines Actions → Delivers Outcomes. IBAOs are commonly written as a company's Purpose, Mission, Vision, and Values/Behaviors, respectively. So, to effectively provide certainty and foster trust through every level of a company, it is essential that the desired Identity, Beliefs, and Actions of each person in the organization are laid out explicitly for a couple of reasons:

1. Each person is aware of what is expected of them during the interview process so they can choose and understand what will be expected of them during each day of their employment.
2. Extreme clarity and visibility make it easier to identify and provide specific feedback at the moment, especially when a Leader or Employee's actions are different from what is expected.

I prefer leveraging the terms Identity and Beliefs because they speak to the behavioral science factors that come into play when leading groups of people. Generally speaking, it is best when the IBAO at work is similar, if not very aligned, to their IBAO outside of work. When I examine Identity and Beliefs for the employee, I focus on their identity at work because it's the one you can initially directly impact as a leader.

Lastly, it is valuable to list your values/behaviors in order of importance. This will help employees by giving them a decision matrix that assists them in consistently choosing the right thing, especially when they face difficult decisions. They will take the action supporting the highest value or behavior level. The power of this practice is that you are choosing the decisions you'll make in the future when you are clear of mind. We can complicate decisions and actions at the moment because of the hormones running through our bodies at the time. Prioritizing your values and behaviors allows you to be confident and clear and to stay in Spirit during pressured moments. You can say, "When I was calm and clear of mind, I intentionally chose these values and behaviors and in this specific order. So now, being in a moment when I feel anxiety, stress and doubt, I can lean on my wisdom when I was at my best self to help me choose."

Let me share a personal story that demonstrates how this can work. I learned this practice of choosing how I would behave from my Bradley Method instructor when I was pregnant with my son. My husband and I were towards the end of our series when we did a "worst case scenario" exercise on fifteen to twenty pieces of paper. We listed scenarios like "partner not in room," "epidural or no epidural," "unable to pulse umbilical cord," "c-section during an emergency," "save mom or save baby," and so on. And we had to sit there and place them in order or priority when we were calm of mind to help us align our identity and beliefs as a team and prepare ourselves for labor and delivery. It allowed us to stay in peace and spirit in a chaotic situation and make the best decisions, regardless of what could happen. It is a phenomenal, proactive practice!

Aligned and Committed Leadership

Through my experiences, I have witnessed that the actions of the leaders are hands-down THE MAKE or BREAK of organizational culture. So when a leader does something different than what is being asked of you, it breaks trust and credibility. Plus, the majority of the time, leaders are not even given direct feedback for these decisions, creating a climate of hypocrisy. They also send a message that there are double standards, and their employees will focus on all the times and moments leaders failed to be who they say they are.

Who you put into key positions and the decisions they make will have a powerful signaling and ripple effect across and down the corporate chain that can either advance or damage culture. I believe all leaders, including the Board of Directors, should be held to the same standard, if not higher, as all employees. There must be a regimented filtering and validation process for leaders to take on roles. The best "tests" are ones where you can observe the person in a high-pressure situation. The "ugly" in us comes out when we are pressured, so it's helpful to see what comes out when a person is stressed. This is not to say that leaders must be perfect. It does mean that leaders must be self-aware, humble, and intentional about their actions and influence.

The prime example of such a process is the Navy Seals. I was privileged to hear former Navy Seal Larry Yatch present at a seminar. He shared with us that only 6% of the tens of thousands of applicants who apply every year meet the requirements. And of that 6%, only about one in five complete the training. As I understand it, many get injured, and some have even died during the process. By no means am I saying all companies should have similar rigor in their selection process because the Navy Seals' line of work is literally life and death. But a significant effort should be made to fiercely protect the culture you want and ensure leaders will be strong ambassadors.

In speaking with HR Leaders across industries, many companies lessened their criteria to get more hires through the door, especially during the COVID pandemic. While that helped keep businesses afloat, it opened the door for employees of different cultures to be brought in. Some companies, however, like Disney, chose to not fill positions if they didn't have the right person to protect their culture.

On average, I estimate about 70% of leaders really want to be aligned and committed and genuinely believe they are. Furthermore, a maximum of 20% of current leaders are aligned and committed to the desired IBAO in most organizations. You may think that's a meager percentage. However, 20% may even be a generous estimate, as Maslow believed that less than 2% of the human population ever attain self-actualization.

Rituals

Rituals are specific actions done daily by all leaders and employees at routine times that serve as reminders of their communal IBAO. A ritual could be saying a particular phrase when greeting each other, leaders working a front-line shift monthly or quarterly, or even starting the workday by reciting your purpose and IBAO.

Once you understand the concept and intent, creating a long list of possible rituals is easy. The key is to filter them down to a few that reinforce critical beliefs, then design them in a way where employees have to be present. Being present during these rituals is important because it allows participants to consciously process what they are doing and why. It allows them the power to choose to believe and act accordingly or not.

I know "rituals" is an odd term to use in a business or work environment since it's generally used in religious contexts. However, self-actualization and purpose are matters of the Spirit, so I think it's absolutely appropriate.

Rituals should be highly unique to an organization, as well as intentional. At first, it may look or feel weird to an outsider, and some might even say the company feels like a cult. Usually, the word cult holds a negative connotation, but having a cult-like culture is a positive thing for purpose-driven organizations. After all, "cult" is the root word in culture.

To add a complementary perspective, Jim Collins states in his article "Building Companies to Last" that "Architects of visionary companies don't just trust in good intentions or 'values statements;' they build cult-like cultures around their core ideologies. Walt Disney created an entire language to reinforce his company's ideology. Disneyland employees are 'cast members.' Customers are 'guests.' Jobs are 'parts' in a 'performance.' Disney required—as the company does to this day—that all new employees go through a 'Disney Traditions' orientation course, in which they learn the company's business is 'to make people happy.'" (Collins 1995)

Environment

Environment means everything that hits our five senses - what people see, feel (externally and emotionally), hear, smell, and taste in their work experience. The environment is a critical factor because how it affects our five senses impacts our focus and emotions. Thus, an environment can derail or reinforce that of a team.

There must be a mandatory process where everything is assessed as advancing or damaging to the desired organizational culture. For example, suppose a company boasts holistic health and well-being for all as a belief or priority. Then the food offerings on site and their employee workload and workday should clearly foster that health and well-being.

As humans, we are programmed to react to our environment. An environment loaded with signals that perpetuate specific actions helps to reinforce the beliefs that drive them. Going back to the above example, employees in this scenario of food offerings are more likely to believe and practice health and well-being because their environment consistently supports that message.

Here is one innovative example of how to incorporate identity and beliefs into the environment and culture. If an organization declares health and well-being are of utmost importance, it needs to ensure that its structure and processes reinforce them. Sounds simple enough, right? Let's take the problem of work-life health or the lack thereof in the US. There are certain activities the average person, as well as practitioners and experts, assert have a direct impact on health and overall well-being. How well does this company protect those activities for its people? I view this as a math problem. You see, there are only twenty-four hours in a day, and every activity we do takes time. Additionally, work-related activities take up a lot of people's hours within a day. So, how do we structure our business, workforce, and operating models so that our people are in the optimal condition to perform? One big way is to ensure the work being asked can actually get done in the time allotted or expected. Take a look at the following grid to see what I mean.

Activity	# Hours Protected
Prepare and eat 3 meals	1.5 Hours
Shower and get dressed	0.5 Hour
House Chores / Errands / Family Needs	1 Hour
Self-Care / Well-being	1 Hour
Relationships	1 Hour
Self-Development	1 Hour
Sleep	8 Hours
Work (including commute)	**10 Hours**
Total	**24 Hours**

On the left, there are minimal activities that we must allow time to do for optimal health and well-being on an average workday. On the right is the number of hours allotted for each activity. Note that in some cases, my estimates are lean. For example, one hour for chores and errands might not be enough time if you have a family versus living by yourself. The math shows that work (including the commute to and from) should be no more than 10 hours of someone's day. Creating an environment that caps work-related activities to 10 hours and allows for recovery and meal breaks throughout the day, as well as relaxation, are things this company could do to uphold its health and well-being belief.

Telling people who are programmed with drive and work ethic to "work less" or to "take time off for yourself" is NOT ENOUGH since there are likely environmental triggers everywhere that command our brains to "work more." It's just like saying "stop snacking" to a serial snacker, then throwing them into a room with all their favorite snacks. This may seem extreme, but I've lived it, and it can feel like torture. Assessing your employees' environment for major triggers or counter messages and relentlessly eliminating them is critical to ensuring your work environment aligns with your culture.

Reinforcement

Another powerful way to leverage our human condition is to employ operant conditioning. Operant conditioning is a type of associative learning where we can encourage or discourage a specific behavior by using positive or negative reinforcement (reward or punishment), respectively.

In a work setting, pay and benefits are one of the most successful tools for reward or punishment. I'm a huge proponent of placing at least equal compensation potential on how employees act and behave rather than on the outcomes they achieve. Reward the direct behavior that is truly desired. An example would be including employee turnover and engagement data as part of performance payout calculations.

Additionally, the means to measure performance must be transparent and applied consistently up the chain. This ensures culture critical behaviors are modeled in a top-down approach. This extreme discipline helps foster trust, especially in cultures that might currently be damaged or broken. In fact, seeing leaders being consistently held accountable for what they expect from their employees gives hope for the future and builds credibility among leaders. On the contrary, inconsistent accountability does incredible damage to the culture and employee morale.

Leading People Through Purpose

One of the biggest challenges purpose-driven organizations try to tackle is getting each employee at every level and down to the front lines to connect to and live the company's purpose. Here's how I break down that dilemma.

Take another look at Maslow's Hierarchy of Needs. Where would you say the leaders (generally medium-level leaders up to C-Suite/Executive Team) trying to solve this problem are personally in the pyramid?

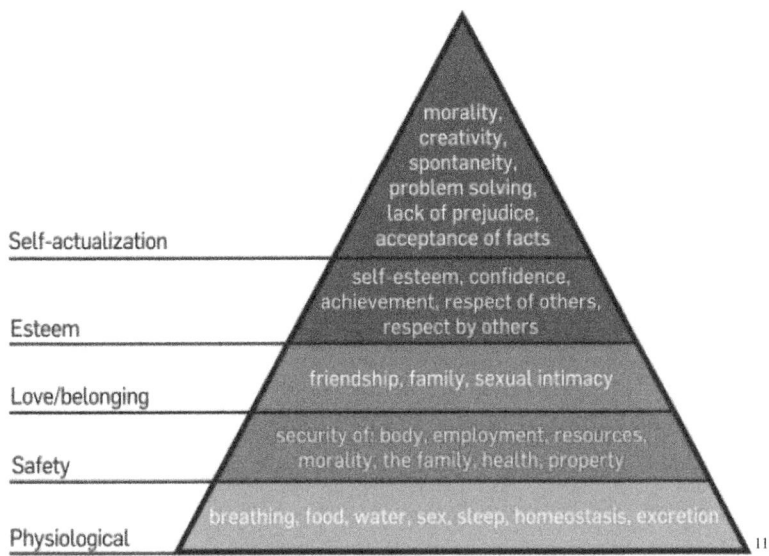

Almost all leaders that I have tested this on answer Esteem and/or Self-Actualization. The correlation to those answers is that they have sufficient resources or experiences to focus on the higher-level areas.

Okay, now where do you think front-line employees are personally in the pyramid?

Almost all people I have tested this on answer somewhere in the bottom three levels. The correlation to these responses is they have fewer resources and experiences and have to focus on the lower-level areas.

If living with purpose is what happens when you self-actualize, then you can truly live out a company purpose when you are at the top of the pyramid. However, Maslow's model opens our eyes to the fact that most employees at lower levels are physically, mentally, and emotionally

---

11 Abraham H. Maslow, *A Theory of Human Motivation* (United States: Historical Recordings, 2020), cover art.

incapable of comprehending and living a purpose because their energy is focused on activities like paying bills, getting food on the table, taking care of their living space, ensuring their children have the things they need, and having healthy relationships.

We can't force or train a person to connect and live with purpose. We can only encourage and inspire them to do so. I believe the way businesses, especially big businesses, can get their employees to live their company purpose is to understand where in the pyramid each employee is and then leverage their benefits and resources to help each self-transform and improve their quality of life up the needs pyramid. Eventually, employees will make their way to self-actualization and discover their own personal life purpose. And if it aligns with the company's purpose, they can co-create together for the greater good of others through its products and offerings. And if it doesn't align, the employee can choose to find another avenue that co-exists with their vision and help them grow and thrive as an individual, which in turn will help strengthen that company's brand reputation and attract future hires.

Some entrepreneurs deter people from working for companies because "you're making someone else's dreams come true" instead of your own. I think it's only an issue if you are, in fact, sacrificing your dreams. I live for win-wins and the best scenario of helping someone else build their dreams while building your own at the same time.

Once a company's executive team identifies and lands on their IBAO, Aligned and Committed Leadership, Rituals, Environment, and Reinforcement, they can create the Employee Value Proposition or EVP. The EVP is what a company uniquely promises employees in exchange for employment. It is inclusive of pay and benefits and much, much more. Gone are the days of the EVP being primarily focused on compensation and benefits, career development, and opportunities. The EVP should be more and more about the employees' experience, work environment, and culture. How does the experience of being with a company enhance your employees' overall life experience? Is it helping you elevate them to their greatest level of self-expression? I strive to transform companies' employee value proposition questions from "What am I getting?" to "Who am I becoming?" I ask, "What kind of people are you nurturing?" and "How are you specifically and intentionally helping them to become greater?"

Below, you will see a visual of how to apply Maslow's Hierarchy of Needs to a generic Employee Value Proposition model.

Employee Value Proposition Example

We Want Team Members Who Personally Connect to Our Purpose and Share Our Identity; Their Basic Needs Must First be Met

Transformation is every Person's responsibility.

As a Business, we exist to assist every person with their needs to enable self-transformation. Primarily we help solve a need with the product/service we provide as a business.

As THE Employer of Choice, our duty is to provide our Employees the environment and resources that assist them in meeting their needs, so they can self-transform and, ultimately, find and pursue their unique life purpose.

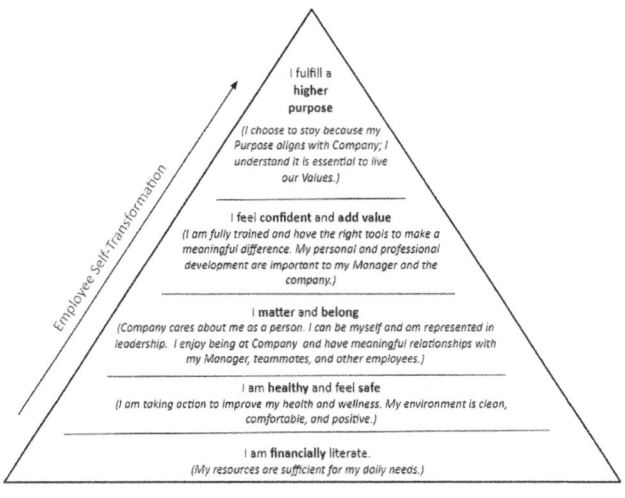

12 Maslow's Hierarchy of Needs pyramid, applied to an Employee Value Proposition (EVP) framework, n.d.

The best time to induct employees into company culture is during the orientation process. Most companies' orientations last only one day. I dare to suggest that companies allow at least one week for colleagues to learn, explore, and process culture and the resources personally available to them. Mind you, this is all before onboarding begins. Yet, prioritizing this sends a strong message that what matters most to you as a leader is them.

My Bold Belief

You CANNOT be purpose and values-driven and equally be about money. Point blank. Period. At some point, this world will force you to choose to validate who you are and what you stand for. Your IDENTITY & BELIEFS are revealed through your decisions and actions. And you tell the world and others every day who you are. And so the question then becomes, "Are you aware of who you are being?"

My Bold Dream for America

I dream that one day there will be a CEO who is bold, brave, and mentally and spiritually FREE from the perceived power of money to where they can lead a publicly traded company towards an abundance of resources by keeping its company's purpose and values a priority over profits.

Unbecoming Reference Material

Here are the main concepts for Unbecoming all in one place.

Becoming, Unbecoming, and Being: When Becoming is not working, try Unbecoming. When you get really good at Unbecoming and revert back to your child-like state, you'll find you can begin to access Being. This simple graphic representation, introduced in "Understanding Unbecoming," illustrates its most basic principles.

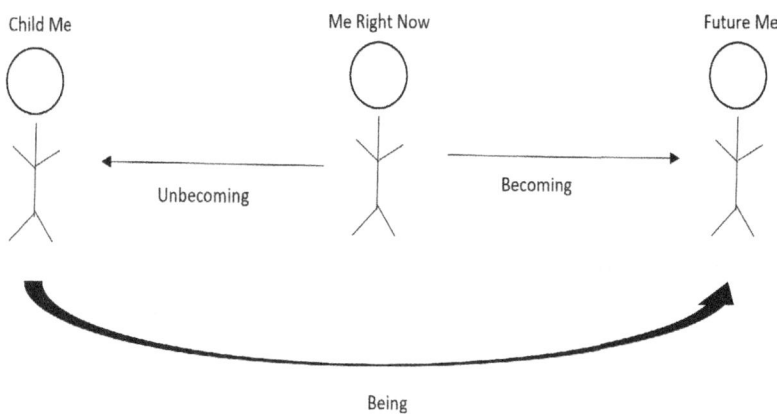

Two Main Identities: It is very easy throughout the day to forget we are spiritual beings having a human experience. Use the following grid from the "Our Duality" chapter to observe how you're showing up at any given moment or over a period of time and identify when and how often you're acting as your Spirit or Human self.

Two Main Identities	
Spirit	**Human**
Authentic	Inauthentic
Divine	Worldly
Infinite	Finite
Live	Exist/Don't Die
Love	Lust/Control
Giving/Service	Getting/Ego
Create	Consume
Needs	Wants
Abundance	Scarcity
Win-Win/Collaboration	Win-Lose/Competition
Gratitude	Jealousy
Forgiveness	Offense
Security	Insecurity
Faith - Focus on the Promise; Embrace Struggle	Fear - Focus on the Pain; Avoid Struggle
Peace	Pain/Suffering
Lifted/Free	Weighed Down/Tethered
Joy (Intrinsic)	Happiness (Extrinsic)
Adventure	Safety
Awe/Wonder of the "Ordinary"	Increased Stimulation
Progress	Perfection
Growth Mindset	Fixed Mindset
Emotional Feeling (Internal)	Five Senses (External)
Impact	Achievement
Holy	Healthy
Present Moment & Energy	Money

Physiological Self-Assessment: Use the grid to assess where you are today compared to your Newborn State. See the potential healing activities for suggested actions. Also, consider partnering with your medical doctor, naturopathic doctor, therapist, and other experts to understand what else you can do to return your body to these optimal states. Please refer back to the "Physiological" chapter for more information.

Newborn State	Your Current State? Y/N	Potential Healing Activity
Breathing from Diaphragm		Daily belly breathing exercise
Flexibility		Yoga, stretching, weekly chiropractor visits, monthly massage appointment
Fluids throughout the day		Half to one ounce of water per pound of weight daily, a bit of sea salt in water as an electrolyte
Getting sufficient sleep		7-9 hours a day, practice 4-7-8 breathing at bedtime
Processing food/ expelling waste after each meal		High nutrient and whole/ unprocessed foods when able, 5 servings of fruits & vegetables daily (smoothies), intermittent fasting, minimize animal meat or products, regular prebiotics and probiotics, detoxes/cleanses
Enjoying being and not preoccupied/ stress		Meditation, therapy, coaching, motivational videos and/or songs, affirmations, limiting distractions, focus on things that bring you joy, moderate to strenuous physical activity while listening to slow-paced music, exploring nature, acupuncture, sound healing, herbs, and supplements (check with a Naturopathic Doctor)

Unbecoming and Maslow's Hierarchy of Needs: This visual, derived from psychologist Abraham Maslow's original pyramid and first discussed in the "Maslow's Hierarchy of Needs" chapter, lays out the five levels of people's needs as initially created by him. Maslow asserts we have an innate desire to fulfill each need, starting at the bottom. We then elevate up. Unbecoming is an intentional practice of reconnecting with and activating our Spirit self, which is needed to self-actualize.

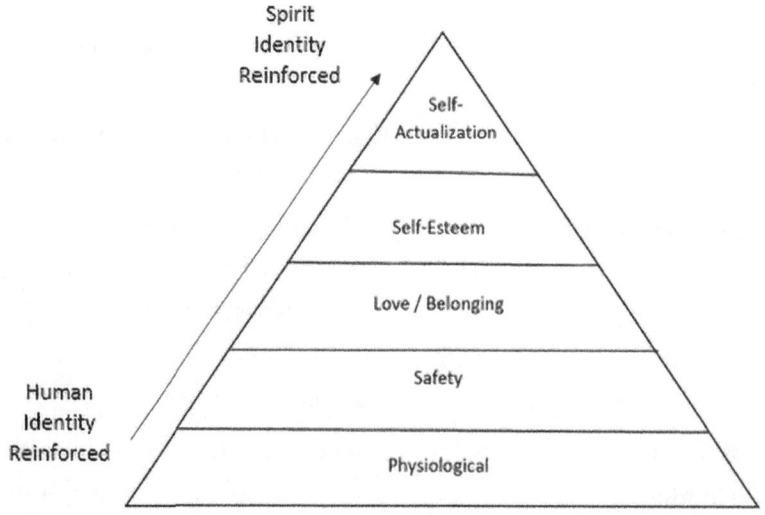

"Maslow's Hierarchy of Needs and Our Duality": From this chapter, the grid below articulates the Human and Spirit traits that correlate with each level of Maslow's Hierarchy of Needs. The goal is to be aware of which identity we are acting out at any given moment, then adjust accordingly if it's not who we want to be.

Human	Maslow's Hierarchy	Spirit
	Self-Actualization & Purpose	Divine, Giving, Faith, Freedom, Intuition, Impact, Holy, Present in the moment, Energy, Living, Awe/Wonder, Holy
Worldly, Getting, Fear, Weighed Down, Five Senses, Finite, Consume, Wants, Pain, Happiness, Perfection, Fixed Mindset, Achievement, Not present, Money	Esteem, Career, & Achievement	Infinite, Create, Needs, Peace, Joy, Progress, Growth Mindset, Healthy
Inauthentic, Lust/Control, Competition, Jealousy, Offense	Love/Belonging	Authentic, Love, Collaboration, Gratitude, Forgiveness,
Insecurity, Adventure	Safety	Security, Safety
Existing, Stimulation, Healthy	Physiological	

IBAO Grid: IBAO stands for Identity, Beliefs, Actions, and Outcome. As discussed in the "Self-Actualization and Purpose" chapter, the Outcome of any situation and our quality of experience is created from the Actions we take. The Actions we take are prompted by the Beliefs (mostly subconscious ones) we hold. And the Beliefs we hold directly align with how we see ourselves, our Identity. This grid is a way to reflect and discover your subconscious beliefs and identity from your upbringing and prior experiences, then consciously create the beliefs and identity that foster a desired state.

	Desired State	Current State
Outcome		
Action		
Belief		
Identity		

Employee Value Proposition (EVP) Model: This is an example of how one can apply Maslow's Hierarchy of needs to an EVP framework, as discussed in "Applying Maslow's Hierarchy to Business Strategy."

We Want Team Members Who Personally Connect to Our Purpose and Share Our Identity; Their Basic Needs Must First be Met
   Transformation is every Person's responsibility.
As a Business, we exist to assist every person with their needs to enable self-transformation. Primarily we help solve a need with the product/service we provide as a business.

As THE Employer of Choice, our duty is to provide our Employees the environment and resources that assist them in meeting their needs, so they can self-transform and, ultimately, find and pursue their unique life purpose.

Recommended Reading and Resources

These are readings and resources that have been insightful for my own Unbecoming and self-transformation towards my Spirit self. I'm sharing them in the chance that even one of them may be of service to you as well.

Physiological
- The Power of Full Engagement: Managing Energy, Not Time, Is the Key to High Performance and Personal Renewal by Jim Loehr and Tom Schwartz
- The Mind-Gut Connection: How the Hidden Conversation Within Our Bodies Impacts Our Mood, Our Choices, and Our Overall Health by Emeran Mayer, MD
- Medical Medium by Anthony William
- Medical Medium: Life-Changing Foods by Anthony William

Financial Safety
- American Consumer Credit Counseling at www.consumercredit.com
- Financial Peace by Dave Ramsey and Sharon Ramsey
- The Total Money Makeover: A Proven Plan for Financial Fitness by Dave Ramsey
- Rich Dad Poor Dad - What the Rich Teach Their Kids About Money by Richard Kiyosaki
- Rich Dad's Cashflow Quadrant: Guide to Financial Freedom by Richard Kiyosaki
- MONEY Master the Game: 7 Simple Steps to Financial Freedom by Tony Robbins
- Unshakeable: Your Financial Freedom Playbook by Tony Robbins and Peter Mallouk

Love and Belonging
- The 5 Love Languages: The Secret to Love that Lasts by Gary Chapman

- Sacred Marriage: What if God Designed Marriage to Make Us More Holy Than to Make Us More Happy? by Gary Thomas
- The Awakened Family: How to Raise Empowered, Resilient, and Conscious Children by Shefali Tsabary, Ph.D.

Esteem, Career, and Achievement

- The Last Lecture by Randy Pausch and Jeffrey Zaslow
- How to Interview Like a Badass: The Comprehensive Guide to Finding and Securing the Job of Your Dreams by Latoya Baldwin
- I Declare: 31 Promises to Speak Over Your Life by Joel Osteen
- DISC Assessment at https://www.discprofile.com/what-is-disc/disc-styles
- Marcus Buckingham's StandOut Assessment at https://mailchi.mp/marcusbuckingham.com/standout-assessment
- Strengths Finder 2.0: A New and Upgraded Edition of the Online Test from Gallup's Now Discover your Strengths by Tom Rath
- The Enneagram Institute's RHETI® Test at https://tests.enneagraminstitute.com

Self-Actualization and Purpose

- The Alchemist by Paolo Coelho
- Landmark Forum by Landmark Worldwide at https://www.landmarkworldwide.com/ the-landmark-forum
- Advanced Course by Landmark Worldwide at https://www.landmarkworldwide.com/ advanced-programs/the-landmark-advanced-course
- Tony Robbins Leadership Academy at https://www.tonyrobbins.com/events/leadership-academy/leadership-academy-virtual/
- Tony Robbins Results Coaching at https://www.tonyrobbins.com/coaching/results-life-coach/
- Tony Robbins The Time of Your Life Program at https://store.tonyrobbins.com/products/the-time-of-your-life
- Success is Natural: with Practical Benefits of Spirituality by Rohit Chauhan

Bibliography

American Consumer Credit Counseling. Accessed November 1, 2022. https://www.consumercredit.com/.

Baldwin, Latoya. *How to Interview Like a Badass: The Comprehensive Guide to Finding and Securing the Job of Your Dreams.* United States: Robinson Anderson Publishing, 2021.

Buckingham, Marcus. "StandOut: Discover Your Strengths." Created with MailChimp. Accessed June 21, 2023. https://mailchi.mp/marcusbuckingham.com/standout-assessment.

Chapman, Gary. *The 5 Love Languages: The Secret to Love that Lasts.* United States: Moody Publishers, 2014.

Chauhan, Rohit. *Success Is Natural: With Practical Benefits of Spirituality.* n.p.: CreateSpace Independent Publishing Platform, 2017.

Coelho, Paulo. *The Alchemist.* United Kingdom: HarperCollins, 2006.

Collins, Jim. "Building Companies to Last." 1995. https://www.jimcollins.com/article_topics/ articles/building-companies.html.

DiSCProfile. "DiSC styles." Accessed June 21, 2023. https://www.discprofile.com/ what-is-disc/disc-styles.

The Enneagram Institute Testing Center. Accessed June 21, 2023. https://tests.enneagraminstitute.com.

Hall, John E. "States of Brain Activity - Sleep, Brain Waves, Epilepsy, Psychoses." In *Guyton and Hall Textbook of Medical Physiology, 12th Ed.* United Kingdom: Elsevier Saunders, 2011.

Healthline. "The 6 Best Ways to Rehydrate Quickly." Medically reviewed by Danielle Hildreth, RN, CPT and Gavin Van De Walle,

MS, RD. Updated on May 23, 2023. https://www.healthline.com/nutrition/how-to-rehydrate#5.-Oral-hydration-solutions.

Himalayan Yoga Institute. "Ujjayi Breath – Blessing or Curse?" Accessed November 1, 2022. https://www.himalayanyogainstitute.com/ujjayi-breath-blessing-curse/.

Huapala. "Iesu Me Ke Kanaka Waiwai (Jesus and The Rich Man) - music by John K. Almeida." Accessed November 1, 2022. https://www.huapala.org/Ia/Iesu_Me_Ke_Kanaka.html.

Innobatics Business and Life Growth. "The Pyramid of Human Needs and the Path to Self-Actualization." Accessed November 1, 2022. https://innobatics.gr/en/maslow-pyramid-of-needs/#:~:text=Maslow%20estimated%20that%20only%202%25%2 0of%20people%20can,of%20the%20obstacles%20which%20stop%20 all%20the%20oth ers.

Jang, Yunjeong. "Artefacts using human brainwaves." MA/MFA Computational Arts blog, Goldsmiths, University of London. Accessed 11/1/2022. http://doc.gold.ac.uk/ compartsblog/index.php/work/artefacts-using-human-brainwaves/.

Kiyosaki, Robert T. *Rich Dad's Cashflow Quadrant: Guide to Financial Freedom*. United States: Plata Publishing, 2011.

Kiyosaki, Robert T. *Rich Dad Poor Dad - What the Rich Teach Their Kids About Money*. Germany: Zack Bowman, 2021.

Kumar, Karthik MBBS. "How Much Water Should You Drink Based on Your Weight?" MedicineNet. February 1, 2023. https://www.medicinenet.com/ how_much_water_to_drink_based_on_your_weight/article.htm.

Kwong, Emily. "Understanding Unconscious Bias." NPR. July 15, 2020. https://www.npr.org/2020/07/14/891140598/understanding-unconscious-bias.

Landmark Worldwide. "Advanced Course." Accessed November 1, 2022. https://www.landmarkworldwide.com/advanced-programs/the-landmark-advanced-course.

Landmark Worldwide. "The Landmark Forum." Accessed November 1, 2022. https://www.landmarkworldwide.com/the-landmark-forum.

Loehr, Jim, and Tony Schwartz. *The Power of Full Engagement: Managing Energy, Not Time, Is the Key to High Performance and Personal Renewal.* United Kingdom: Free Press, 2003.

Maslow, Abraham Harold. *Motivation and Personality.* United Kingdom: Harper & Row, 1954. Maslow, Abraham Harold (1943) "A Theory of Human Motivation." *Psychological Review.* 50 (4): 370–96. 1943. Posted August 2000 on Classics in the History of Psychology. psychclassics.yorku.ca/Maslow/motivation.htm.

Mayer, Emeran MD. *The Mind-Gut Connection: How the Hidden Conversation Within Our Bodies Impacts Our Mood, Our Choices, and Our Overall Health.* New York: Harper Wave, 2016.

New World Encyclopedia. "File: Maslow's Hierarchy of Needs.Svg." December 19, 2007. https://www.newworldencyclopedia.org/p/index.php?title=File%3AMaslow%27s_hierarch y_of_needs.svg.

Osteen, Joel. *I Declare: 31 Promises to Speak Over Your Life.* United States: FaithWords, 2012. Pausch, Randy, and Zaslow, Jeffrey. *The Last Lecture.* Australia: Hachette Australia, 2010.

Psychology Discussion. "Functions of Reticular Activating System (RAS) | Brain | Neurology." Accessed November 30, 2022. https://www.psychologydiscussion.net/brain/ functions-of-reticular-activating-system-ras-brain-neurology/2893.

Ramsey, Dave. *The Total Money Makeover: A Proven Plan for Financial Fitness*. United States: Thomas Nelson, 2009.

Ramsey, Dave, and Ramsey, Sharon. *Financial Peace*. United States: Lampo Group Inc. 1995.

Rath, Tom. *Strengths Finder 2.0: A New and Upgraded Edition of the Online Test from Gallup's Now Discover your Strengths*. United States: Gallup Press, 2007.

Robbins, Tony. "GET YOUR WINNING EDGE: Tony Robbins Results Coaching." Tony Robbins. Accessed November 1, 2022. https://www.tonyrobbins.com/coaching/results-life-coach/.

Robbins, Tony. "LEADERSHIP ACADEMY." Tony Robbins. Accessed November 1, 2022. https://www.tonyrobbins.com/events/leadership-academy/leadership-academy-virtual/.

Robbins, Tony. *MONEY Master the Game: 7 Simple Steps to Financial Freedom*. United States: Simon & Schuster, 2016.

Robbins, Tony. "The Time of Your Life." Tony Robbins. Accessed November 1, 2022. https://store.tonyrobbins.com/products/the-time-of-your-life.

Robbins, Tony, and Mallouk, Peter. *Unshakeable: Your Financial Freedom Playbook*. United States: Simon & Schuster, 2018.

Rohn, Jim. "The Real Value in Setting Goals." Success Presents Jim Rohn International. August 30, 2019. https://www.jimrohn.com/get-inspired-by-your-goals/.

Sheridan, Mary D., Sharma, Ajay, and Frost, Marion. *From Birth to Five Years: Children's Developmental Progress*. United Kingdom: Taylor & Francis, 2002.

Tan, Flora. "Two Wolves - A Cherokee Story - also known as Grandfather Tells and The Wolves Within." A-Simple-Christian.com. Accessed November 1, 2022. https://www.a-simple-christian.com/two-wolves.html.

Thomas, Gary. *Sacred Marriage: What If God Designed Marriage to Make Us Holy More Than to Make Us Happy?* United States: Zondervan, 2015.

Tsabary, Shefali. *The Awakened Family: How to Raise Empowered, Resilient, and Conscious Children.* United States: Penguin Publishing Group, 2017.

Walker, Ronald D., and Eleanor J. Gibson. "The Visual Cliff." *Scientific American.* 202 (4) 64-71. April 1, 1960. https://doi.org/10.1038/scientificamerican0460-64.

William, Anthony. *Medical Medium Life-Changing Foods: Save Yourself and the Ones You Love with the Hidden Healing Powers of Fruits & Vegetables.* United States: Hay House, 2016.

William, Anthony. *Medical Medium Revised and Expanded Edition: Secrets Behind Chronic and Mystery Illness and How to Finally Heal.* United Kingdom: Hay House, 2016.

Williamson, Marianne. *A Return to Love: Reflections on the Principles of A Course in Miracles.* United States: HarperCollins, 2009.

Young, Melissa, MD. "How To Do the 4-7-8 Breathing Exercise." Cleveland Clinic. September 6, 2022. https://health.clevelandclinic.org/4-7-8-breathing/.

About the Author

Rowen Labuguen Turner is a Fortune 5 trained Business Leader, Leadership and Culture Innovator, Real Estate Investor, and Author of *Unbecoming*.

As a Filipina-American, Rowen was born and raised in Honolulu, Hawaii, where her immigrant parents and grandparents instilled in her the importance of Faith, Family, and Education. Church and family gatherings are key memories of her childhood. Leadership is also a big part of Rowen's life. She has consistently taken on leadership roles since she was eight, ranging from student ministry to student government. This led to formal roles in business, as well as informal leadership roles within her community. Having been raised in a relatively strict home, Rowen doesn't recall what interested her about becoming a leader. But as she grew older, taking on leadership activities became an effective way to get outside-of-school time with her friends and, along with her education and social awareness, led to her being the effective leader she is today.

Rowen has a BA in Biology and an MBA with an emphasis in Corporate Strategy from the University of Hawaii at Manoa. For about fourteen years, she focused her energy within the Human Resources arena and is certified as a Senior Professional in Human Resources (SPHR). She currently serves as Chief Purpose and Operating Officer for The Multifamily Mindset, a real estate business consulting company. Her greatest impact lies in leading teams to achieve breakthrough and sustainable results through leadership and culture transformation. Additionally, she serves other leaders and entrepreneurs through her coaching and consulting business.

Core to her Filipino background and Hawaiian upbringing is her love for great food and the outdoors. While Rowen is a "social butterfly," she values connection time with loved ones and regular, quiet-minded "me" time. She is fascinated with self-development, specifically with how the body, mind, and spirit are interconnected and how we can apply that knowledge as individuals to morph our current reality and create our dream lives. She is also focused on applying that knowledge to leaders within organizations so that their team members can learn and do the same.

Rowen's mission is to change the world by transforming Life's question from "What am I getting?" to "Who am I *Unbecoming?*." Her greatest message is to encourage others to connect with their Spirit self and to explore an active and intentional relationship with God.

Rowen currently lives in Orlando, Florida, with her husband Marcus and their two sons, Myles (5) and Jett (3).

You can stay connected with Rowen and more Unbecoming resources by visiting her at:

- www.unbecomingRLT.com
- Instagram: coachrow_unbecoming

Made in the USA
Middletown, DE
05 May 2024

53899296R00116